PILOTING

YOUR

LIFE

PILOTING

YOUR

LIFE

TERRI HANSON MEAD

PILOTING YOUR LIFE

Non Fiction

Text copyright ©2019 by Terri Hanson Mead

Cover designed by Seedlings Online at www.seedlingsonline.com
Ebook production by E-books Done Right at www.ebooksdoneright.com
Typesetting by Atthis Arts at www.atthisarts.com

Every effort has been made to ensure that the content provided herein is accurate, up-to-date, and helpful to the reader at the time of publication. However, this is not intended to replace or treat any conditions, nor is it an exhaustive treatment of the subject. We encourage anyone to seek help with a professional counselor, therapist, or healthcare professional where issues deem it necessary. No liability is assumed. The reader is considered responsible for your choices, actions, and results undertaken after reading this work.

Visit www.PilotingYourLife.com for more information about the author, updates, or new books.

ISBN: 9781086471922 (paperback)
        9781393647225 (ebook)

FOR REI AND ADAM

FOR BEING MY TRUE NORTH.

CONTENTS

MIDLIFE IS AN OPPORTUNITY, NOT A CRISIS

The phrase *midlife crisis*, coined by Elliott Jaques in an article in 1965, never really applied to women. Women, because of pregnancy, hormones, menopause, and, well, just being *women*, weren't included in his research. *Midlife crisis* was a catchy phrase that caught on in a way it was never meant to, and later research showed that only 10% of men actually experience midlife crisis.

So, it's *really* not a thing.

I don't think I even knew the term *midlife* until I was forty-eight, a full eight years into it. (Midlife is the time between forty and sixty-five.)

At forty-eight, I knew that I was suffering from feeling dismissed and overlooked professionally and personally. I had experienced weight gain over a one-year period that I couldn't keep blaming on the fallout of the 2016 elections (too much alcohol and cheese), and I kept looking at my body wondering what the fuck had happened. I'd also spent several years looking for greater meaning in my life and two solid years craving sex. I was wondering if this was my new *normal*.

All of these experiences are typical for a lot of women in midlife.

I reject the notion of *crisis* and insert the idea of *opportunity*. Crisis implies something short and sudden. That's not what's really experienced in midlife—which is more like malaise, angst, general unhappiness, or just feeling off-balance.

Midlife isn't a single moment or turning point. It's more of a protracted period of time with the opportunity to take time for you, resolve unresolved childhood and adolescent issues, explore, and experiment as you define your life journey.

Midlife is an opportunity for renewal as we experience a form of "puberty" along with our teenagers (if you have them).

With this opportunity for renewal, we can define what we want the next half of our lives to be, over a comfortable chunk of time. We can play around with old ideas we rejected when we were younger and see what they feel like now. We can explore new territory and see what resonates.

Our lives and bodies are shifting, so why not shift with them?

During this time of exploration and play, it's all about learning. There's no failure, only opportunity to learn and grow. That's why this book is so important. It's meant to remove all taboos and normalize conversations about midlife, menopause, aging, ambition, money, and sex.

MIDLIFE PUBERTY?

So much is changing for us women in midlife . . . our bodies, our minds, our lives. Midlife puberty is an interesting time, and I know a lot of us are completely unprepared for it because we don't talk about it. There's not enough written about it.

We are where we are . . . so let's start talking about it!

I can't tell you the number of times I've read or heard the same phrase from women in midlife: *I thought I was the only one going through this.* Many of us feel isolated and alone, but we needn't feel this way. Our pelvic floors get weaker, so jumping jacks and trampolines may be a thing of the past. Hot flashes are real; they're physiological evidence of an internal change that women go through.

We shouldn't be embarrassed.

We can let go of what no longer serves us, release rules we no longer want, and be curious and optimistic about what comes next. With this book, I want to reignite your spark (if you've lost it) and help you find a way to live *your* life and your soul's purpose.

If you're feeling off-balance, if you're questioning everything, if you're looking in the mirror and seeing a stranger, you're not alone. If you have zero patience for toxicity and following the rules, you are not alone. I am right there with you.

Feel what you're feeling without judgment.

You are not lost. You are where you are . . . which is right where I recommend starting.

GEN X?

Speaking of feeling lost.

An infographic from a program that aired on January 11, 2019 titled *Generation Guidelines Defined by Birth Year* showed the following:

The Silent Generation: Born 1928-1945
Baby Boomers: Born 1946-1964
Millennials: Born 1981-1996
Gen Z: Born 1997-Present

Notice anything missing? Like maybe the sixty-five million of us born between 1965 and 1980? Gen X didn't even make the cut as a living generation worth noting by CBSN.

No wonder we feel dismissed and neglected! Our generation isn't on anyone's radar. We are sandwiched between two outsized generations that think we are totally screwed up.

My lovely Gen Xers, this book on midlife is written especially for you.

WHY I WROTE THIS BOOK

When I was forty-two and forty-three, I didn't know that I felt friskier in the bedroom due to an increase in hormones. As if my body was saying, "If you want to have another baby, now is the time. This is a going-out-of-business sale, and you are soon going to be out of the baby-making business."

When I was forty-five and started looking for more meaningful work, I had no idea that was typical for midlife women, especially those of us in our mid-forties. It didn't occur to me to seek help other than questioning people I knew as I looked for a new professional outlet.

When I was forty-seven and started putting on weight at a steady clip, I didn't know that it was probably due to a decrease in estrogen and that I should make some lifestyle changes because losing weight during the menopause transition is tough for a lot of women.

The list goes on and on.

Midlife blindsided me; I was totally unprepared for it. No one told me what to expect. No one told me how to prepare. No one told me how to take advantage of it. As I opened up to other women about some of these things, I learned I was not alone and decided to do something about it.

I started by talking with other women. I listened to their stories and quickly realized that, while midlife is different for all women, we can connect through our stories and our experiences. I interviewed over thirty-five diverse women from around the world and discovered the universality of our experiences. It crosses borders, gender identity, cultural identity, marital status, parental situation, spirituality, and skin color.

The women I interviewed are straight, gay, single, married, divorced, widowed, black, brown, white, non-white, cisgender, transgender, religious, atheist, spiritual, American, European, New Zealanders, Canadian, and African. Some are moms, and some are not. Some work outside the homes, and others do not. These women are in their forties, fifties, sixties, and seventies. I intentionally left these descriptors out of the stories; I want you to relate on a human and female level, without the distraction of labels.

My goal is to give you diverse stories from a myriad of life experiences and backgrounds to create connections to other women like you.

I want you to know that you are not alone.

There are books on specific topics like happiness, finding your *why*, menopause, money, divorce, parenting, and sex, but nothing that gathers all aspects of our midlives into one place. I conducted extensive research on the topics in this book to provide an umbrella.

Think of *Piloting Your Life* as a *Fodor's* or *Frommer's* guidebook for midlife women. Because, *really*, midlife is an adventure worth exploring.

SHARING THE WEALTH

I had no idea that when I started this book, I would be going on my own personal development and enlightenment journey. I was forty-eight and married with two children. I had a successful IT consulting company in the San Francisco Bay Area, had been angel investing in early-stage startups for over three years, and was advising various startups around the world. I'd worked with my executive coach, Bev, on and off for fifteen years and with other life coaches as needs arose. For me, every day is an opportunity for improvement—but this time, I wanted to do something to help other women, specifically those in midlife. And the more I learned, the more compelled I felt to share the wealth of knowledge.

The desire to write a book to embolden women over the age of forty to take the controls and be the pilots in their own lives drove me. I had a title that tied into my brand as a commercially rated helicopter pilot, a catchy subtitle, a writing coach, and a timeline, and I got right to work on the research. I didn't overthink it. As with most of my best decisions, not *overthinking it* was exactly the right thing for me to do.

WHAT TO EXPECT WHEN . . .

I want you to read this book and feel inspired by the women who make up the bulk of its pages. Hopefully, it will motivate you to make good choices for *you*. May it help you know that being selfish and choosing *you* are your moral imperatives.

Being selfish isn't bad; it's healthy.

And if you aren't quite there yet, I don't want you to be blindsided by midlife. I still ask my older friends why they didn't tell me what to expect. Everyone seems to have an opinion or thought about every other aspect of our lives—why not midlife? There's *What to Expect When You're Expecting* for when we're pregnant, plus *What to Expect the First Year, What to Expect the Second Year,* and more.

What about *What to Expect When You Turn Forty and Slide into Midlife?*

Well, here it is, except with more inspiration and less doom and gloom.

DISENGAGE AUTOPILOT

Despite being a commercially rated helicopter pilot (a girl has to have a hobby!), every time I fly helicopters, I'm afraid . . . but not afraid of what you might think.

I'm afraid I'll screw up on the radio or that I won't hear an instruction from air traffic control. I worry that I won't be able to react safely, legally, and appropriately and that I'll do something that will make someone say, "You aren't qualified to fly."

I've been flying for over ten years. I am afraid, and I still fly.

I am full-on the controls when I fly, just like I try to be in life. There's no autopilot in the helicopters I fly.

So many of us women won't do something if we can't do *all* of it. Or, we stay in something comfortable because it feels easier to be a passenger than to take the controls.

Midlife shouldn't happen on autopilot. We should work through the fear, let go of what no longer serves us, and gain the confidence to design and live the life of our own creation.

Live boldly, my friends.

WHY NOW?

For many women who have been caring for and putting others first, midlife is *the* time when there's finally space to start thinking about you. You may feel compelled to make room for you, to live with greater purpose, or to answer the call to do something big in the world. It's during this time that we can begin to define what legacy we want to leave.

If you've lost sight of who you are and what you want, it's time to explore and experiment and define your own new milestones. Up until this point, there have been socially defined milestones like college, first job, maybe marriage, maybe kids, maybe grad school, maybe the first house, and then if there are kids, the kids' milestones. The lack of milestones can make midlife feel like uncharted territory.

It is, and it's ready to be explored and conquered.

If you're reading this book, it's time. Time for you. Time for vision. Time for clarity. Time for you to resolve unresolved issues from your childhood, adolescence, and early twenties. Because if you don't, they are going to keep resurfacing. Trust me on this one.

TAKING THE CONTROLS

We don't have to suffer during midlife. In fact, I highly recommend using this time of feeling off-balance to take action and begin to take back your life.

At the end of every chapter, there is a **Taking the Controls** section with reflective questions for you to ponder. These are not meant to be prescriptive or exhaustive. We all have our own journeys, and it's up to each of us to own, define, and guide our lives to meet our own needs and desires.

Capture your thoughts in the **Briefing Notes** section, or use the prompts for journaling or chatting with your girlfriends. Do whatever feels best for you, knowing these segments exist to help you transform your midlife journey. For more resources for further exploration, check out the In-Flight Resources at www.PilotingYourLife. com. You'll be able to pull this all together in your own personal **Flight Plan** at the end of the book. Or not.

You get to choose your own adventure.

Because we need friends and deep relationships to keep our brains healthy and our hearts happy, I suggest putting together your own personal crews to serve different purposes in your life. Talking about what we're going through will help us feel less isolated and alone, and we'll begin to normalize conversations around midlife. Check out **Crew Chats** in the Appendix for ways to get started and what to expect. Think of it as your *Table Topics*, but for midlife women with more wine, champagne, laughter, crying, and maybe a little peeing your pants.

As some chapters of our lives are ending, others are just beginning, and we have the opportunity to create what we want for the next half of our lives.

It's time to begin.

Starting with this book.

CHAPTER 1

JOURNEY

While talking with a friend about how all of us have circuitous and serpentine life routes, an image of the Life board game popped into my mind. I used to love playing it when I was younger. Now, I just find it frustrating as it takes so long to play. Even so, it seemed like the best analogy to pull into the book here.

Let's assume we start at the point in the game when we're alone in the little car. Pick your peg color. Pink or blue. Off you go with the first spin of the spinner. In the game, you'll pick up passengers along the way in the form of a spouse and/or kids. You'll draw cards to determine your career, any extra earnings, and payments. The goal is to move from space to space as you head toward the final stop: *Retirement*.

I'd like to see a more modern version of this game with other colored pegs. Let's bring in other realities like death and divorce. (I suppose that would ruin a game for kids.)

We still have half our lives left to live when we reach midlife. Thinking about decades of open terrain can be terrifying and overwhelming. If you think about it too much, it can send you into an anxious spiral.

In reality, life is a game of chance, luck, and effort that unfolds daily. It begins with birth and ends with death. In between, it's a wild ride of opportunities shaped by our families, our environment, and how we handle what's offered.

Earlier in our lives, standard societal milestones keep us on a predictable path. In midlife, the field opens up, and we encounter wide, open terrain that lasts for decades. It becomes up to us to gauge our progress and personal success. *We* define the checkpoints. This can be quite intimidating. Most of us don't acknowledge this wide-open space and want the unidentified and unnamed discomfort to just *go away already*.

What if we broke midlife (and the rest of our lives) down into five- or ten-year segments? Wouldn't that make it easier to manage? We can have long-term plans, but we don't have to have everything figured out.

How do you eat an elephant? One bite at a time. Have no idea where to start? Hold tight; I have ideas for you in some of the later chapters.

As you begin to rethink and reframe your midlife—and the rest of your life—here are some things to keep in mind:

- It's a journey, not a pivot.
- As one chapter ends, another chapter is just beginning.
- Anchors provide stability in times of change and transition.
- You have to be willing to step into the unknown.
- It's worth the effort.
- All the pieces will come together.

Ready for a deeper dive?

IT'S A JOURNEY, NOT A PIVOT

Four years ago, when I decided that I wanted to do something *more* with my professional life, I took steps toward what I naively called a *pivot*. I assumed that whatever I was working toward would ultimately end in something . . . at which point I would be done. I felt overlooked, dismissed, and frustrated in my professional life. I was afraid I was becoming irrelevant and wouldn't be able to provide for my family, our current lifestyle, our future, and eventually, retirement.

That discomfort needed to die.

So, I tried making those yucky feelings go away by filling my life with lots of activities. Surely, achieving that *one thing*, that *next thing*, would make it all better.

Not so.

Last year at Startup Grind, a conference in my hometown, I bumped into my friend Susan. She asked me, "When is your pivot going to be done? I think you should have an end date."

Startled by the question and the pressure, I boldly said, "Well . . . it'll be done at the end of the year." After that, I started marching toward completing my pivot . . .

. . . until I completely forgot about the commitment.

Fast forward a few months. I'm interviewing one of the women for this book, and the topic of pivoting came up. "I'm four-and-a-half years into my pivot," she said. That's when it hit me.

Midlife isn't a pivot.

It's a journey.

I held the delusional belief that if I changed just one thing, all would be well. I wanted to get rid of my midlife angst as quickly as possible and was looking for the magic bullet.

While I'd been working so hard to avoid the uncomfortable feelings, what I really needed to do was stop fighting them and see what they had to tell me. That's hard, by the way. Our minds naturally want to rid themselves of discomfort. We have to fight that natural response and stay with the feelings. We needn't be afraid of losing ourselves in the uncomfortable feelings; it doesn't work that way. In fact, when we sit with them, we tend to discover ourselves.

When my husband and I were deciding when to have children, I kept saying, "I'll be ready when I lose ten pounds." Which morphed into, "I'll be ready after I get this promotion," or "once we have more money saved."

My wise friend Linda said, "There is never *the* ideal time to start a family. Stop waiting, decide, and go for it. You'll only regret it if you keep waiting."

She was right.

The same holds true in midlife. There will never be a perfect time to focus on you. There will always be one more thing to do and one more person to care for. Something will always get in the way of choosing your own path.

It's up to you to make your journey *your* priority. Not later. Now.

Being Intentional

For a lot of women, midlife is when we finally feel free to take time for ourselves.

Jacqueline felt she was in a holding pattern while raising her kids. She loved volunteering in the classroom and leading nature-journaling for second graders, but as her marriage fell apart and her kids grew older, she knew she needed to make changes.

She said, "I didn't know what I wanted to do, and I didn't know where to start. I only knew I didn't want to go back to the career I had before I had kids."

She dabbled in a few things, and with each new experience, she learned and applied her newfound knowledge to the next experience. As the reality of her new situation set in, she knew she needed to be more intentional about making money and building a career. She said, "I wanted to be able to provide for my daughters and create a stronger financial future for myself. I wanted my work to be meaningful and impactful. To do this, I knew I had to take seriously the work of finding work."

Now, with one daughter headed off to college and the other not far behind, Jacqueline has ended her primary focus as a stay-at-home mom. She's shifted her attention to what *she* wants in work, love, and play.

"I feel like I'm just getting started on my journey, and I'm forty-nine!"

Of course, she doesn't have it all figured out. Every day is a new challenge, but she's embracing the change, the opportunities, and looks forward to what's next with hope and excitement rather than fear and avoidance. She is intentional about how she spends her time and where she puts her energy, which brings her closer to what she wants in and out of her life.

The key is to have a deliberate mindset around appreciating where you are (gratitude, anyone?) and optimistically looking forward to what is coming next. This isn't easy. It requires attention to self-care, patience, and finding something stable while everything changes, which brings us to anchors and tie-downs.

ANCHORS AND TIE-DOWNS

In my forties, I made many pivotal decisions, including accepting an invitation to join a group called Change Makers/Rule Breakers for a week on Necker Island, one of Richard Branson's private islands in the British Virgin Islands.

While the island is a beautiful and special place that very few people get to visit, it was the time spent with Richard and the others that led me to search for *more*. At Necker Island, I began to look at the world differently. Having only ever lived in the San Francisco Bay Area, my worldview (and my view of myself) was somewhat limited. Going to Necker changed that for me. And, indirectly, led to this book.

The first invitation came in 2016. I jumped at the chance, booked flights, and sent my payment before I could talk myself out of it.

Despite my fears and misgivings about it being too good to be true, I ended up on the island with thirty amazing people from around the world. I even partnered with Richard Branson on the tennis court.

One day, after lunch on Moskito Island (one of Richard's other private islands), I relaxed on a lounge chair and gazed out across the sparkling, aquamarine channel. A deserted island on the other side beckoned. I could almost hear it saying, "Swim to me, Terri."

Who can resist that?

I didn't tell anyone. I didn't know how I would get back. I just took off my cover-up, left it on the lounge chair, walked down to the water, and started swimming. While swimming, I glanced back a few times to see if anyone was calling me to turn back. At the halfway point, I let go of the pull back to the safety of Moskito Island and kept going.

Three-quarters of the way across, I realized I would be too tired to swim back. I didn't worry about it; I'd figure that out when I got to the beach. I was within shouting distance of the shore when two men in a small speedboat drove up to the beach and started to unpack their things. I yelled at them to hold up, stepped out of the water (I wish I looked like Bo Derek, but I'm pretty sure I was panting like a swamp thing), and asked if they would give me a ride back to Moskito.

After the two brothers from Florida got over the surprise, one of them said, "Hop in! We'll drive you back."

So, I did.

Back at Moskito, I hopped out and said thank you, and they zipped away as I walked up to the bar for a well-deserved drink. Despite being parched and tired, I felt victorious.

As I swam, I kept looking back for someone to tell me I couldn't swim across the channel. I expected someone to tell me I couldn't be on the deserted beach. With this swim, I realized I didn't need anyone else's permission. This was a powerful moment for me. Permission was mine to give, to myself. With that realization, I cut one of the tie-downs holding me back and moved a few steps closer to the freedom to choose my own path on my journey.

Sometimes we just have to get out of our own way.

When we go through transitional periods like midlife, the work is often difficult. Anchors help us ease into the transition by creating a feeling of certainty. But sometimes anchors aren't what they seem.

In other words, don't confuse anchors with tie-downs.

The definitions of each of these terms are very similar . . . but are actually very different. An anchor provides stability; tie-downs hold you back. If an anchor is keeping you from making progress, over time, it becomes a tie-down.

As I let go of tie-downs and experience turbulence in my life, I've added anchors like daily meditation and stretching, regular communication with friends, and morning pages (daily journaling) to provide me with something constant as everything around me changes. When I start to feel blown about and out of control, I come back to these things. For you, it might be getting out into nature, taking a walk, yoga, or other similarly healthy and grounding activities.

STEP INTO THE UNKNOWN

The *Covey Club Reinvent Yourself* podcast became a big inspiration for me as I conducted my research for this book. Host Lesley Jane Seymour interviews women over the age of fifty who reinvented themselves. She covers everything from a very public firing (Sallie Krawcheck), to an empty nest (Jeannie Ralston), to leaving corporate (Randi Levin), and more.

One of her guests, Louise Phillips Forbes says, "Step into the unknown, and say *yes*. Own who you are, and be willing to show up and do the work. Have faith in the process, and when you follow your passions, one dream will lead to another."

So much becomes unknown and unfamiliar in midlife. That won't change, so we might as well accept the discomfort, experiment, and explore. We can't wave a magic wand and make it just so.

No bippity-boppity-boo for us.

We have to actively take steps, often into the unknown, and see where they lead. Then we take it from there.

BETTER ENDINGS LEAD TO BETTER BEGINNINGS (WE SUCK AT CLOSURE)

As a technical project manager, I find rhythms in every project I manage.

After one ends, I always suffer a post-project dip. I spend so much time and energy successfully delivering a tech project that when it's over, my brain and body don't know what to do. I often have to dig deep into my energy reserves to get the project over the finish line. Once the project is over, my body crashes. I used to ignore the drop in my energy levels, occasionally wondering why I was so tired and distracted and unable to clearly focus on the simplest of tasks. I experienced the same thing when I trained for half marathons in my early forties. The months of training, and the race itself, took their toll on me.

Eventually, I realized what was going on and built recovery time into my schedule for both projects and races. During this recovery time, I was kinder and gentler with myself. I also conducted what I called *mini and informal postmortems*. I looked back on the project or the race and mentally noted what went well and what could have been better.

When I took the time to do this, I cruised through the dips. Re-energizing for the next thing became simple. When I didn't have the *mini and informal postmortem*, my energy lagged. I felt as if something was missing. Yep—sure was. Closure. In hindsight, I should have done this after each birthday, after each of my kids' birthdays, after we moved, and any other time that there was an ending.

We are terrible at endings, and this is not a good thing.

My executive coach, Bev, has talked to me for years about the importance of closure. She says, "We need to take the time to reflect on an activity, project, job, or phase in our life." It's true. We often blow through these things, and I guarantee we suffer as a result.

The writings of a guy named Richard Davis[1], commenting on how his granddaughter was turning thirteen and would be having her Bat Mitzvah, caught my eye. The celebration honored the end of her childhood and the beginning of adulthood in her community. While I'm not particularly religious, I appreciate religious traditions that allow for the honoring of endings and celebration of beginnings.

What struck me was the following:

"We so often dread endings. This may be because we build our lives around what is familiar, and we are frightened by change. When something ends, the things that used to be familiar might become rare or even strange. We might have to change, and that can be the most difficult task of all. Yet, as we have all heard, the only constant is change. If we can learn to think of a time of ending as a time of a new beginning, we might relax, at least a little. Beginnings are often the most rewarding times, for it is often there that growth begins. Each season has an ending leading to the beginning of the next. And out of that constant change comes rest, growth, and life."

I love this. It reframes where we are in midlife when we think so much is behind us or is ending. We may have kids heading off to college. We may lose a loved one. We might not get the same appreciative looks when we walk into a room. We may get laid off from a job that we love. All of this can feel like overwhelming loss . . . but, if we reframe our view to look at what is ahead, and let go of what is comfortable, we can create something perfectly suited to our specific needs and desires.

Our journey is our own game of Life (literally and figuratively). We get to make choices as we move to the next space on a board of *our own creation*. This game of Life comes with our own rules and players. We can choose to pause, take a few steps back, move sideways, or accelerate through the spaces, all at different points in our lives.

It is *our* journey, after all.

All the Pieces Come Together

Each woman is unique in the opportunities available to her and the experiences she's assembled over time, but ultimately all of this comes together to form our own personal mosaic, each beautiful and rich in its own way.

Amy, an entrepreneur from the northwest, said, "Everyone's journey is their own. Each individual will need to take inventory of their elements and ingredients and how they mesh with their own comfort level, desire, and DNA to design and craft their own journey."

The idea that the pieces of our lives come together to create a piece of art like a tiled mosaic, a stained-glass window, or a tapestry is a striking one that I love. Personally, I am aiming for one hell of a tapestry that rivals the Bayeux Tapestry in Normandy, France.

One of my favorite lines from the movie *The Best Exotic Marigold Hotel* says, "Everything will be alright in the *end*. If it's not all right, then it's not yet the *end*."

This is magical and liberating. It means that we don't have to have it all figured out at the start. We can figure it out as we go. We can be optimistic knowing it will all come together just as it should.

This is important. As we are creating and assembling the pieces of our lives, it's difficult to see the bigger picture. We can take a step back to try to get a broader view, but even then, we don't necessarily have all the pieces or the right vantage point. We must have faith in the process and that we are doing our best possible work.

I think about when I decided to write a book in 2016. I had the suggestion of a process and then a topic and a title. In a few weeks, I'd created what I thought was good enough content, shared it with a friend, and ended up completely derailed. I stalled out until I heard a podcast two years later and had more experience as a woman in my forties. Only then did all the pieces come together to create this book.

My friend and fellow author, Connie, said, "At some point, we are able to look back and piece together the path. Until that point, it may not make sense."

It's a good reminder, because eventually it does make sense. Eventually, it all comes together.

It's Worth the Effort

When I interviewed Georgia for this book, she spoke about a venture she's been struggling with for years. "I've had to work hard and have chosen to make sacrifices," she said. "Through it all, though, it has been worthwhile. It's been worth all of the effort. When everything seems to be falling apart, I press on. I've learned to ask for help and share the journey so that I can get out of my crazy brain. With each win, I've gained the confidence to keep moving toward my vision. I will succeed."

It took (and takes) courage for not only Georgia, but for all of us, to press on when the going gets tough or we are uncomfortable or scared. We have to have faith in ourselves, knowing that we are worth the effort. Our lives matter. Our choices matter. And we can be afraid and still go for it.

We may need to be courageous to get to confidence. This pretty much sums up the way we need to approach this journey.

Be courageous, and know it's worth the effort.

TAKING THE CONTROLS

— Am I the top priority in my life?
— What am I looking forward to?
— What are my anchors as I transition through midlife?

BRIEFING NOTES

WHAT WE CAN LEARN FROM THE
MARVELOUS MRS. MAISEL

I discovered the Amazon Prime original, *The Marvelous Mrs. Maisel* last year and loved it from the very first episode. It's a quick and witty show that's beautifully staged and costumed, with great lessons for women who want to reinvent themselves—or find themselves in a situation where they have to. That's where the protagonist, Midge, finds herself in the first episode.

Here are the lessons I gleaned:

- **Sometimes, unexpectedly doing something leads to something else that resonates.** Or it may open an unexpected path. Taking a step down the path can help us see what opportunities present themselves, even if it seems like a ridiculous path at first.
- **Be open to imagining without limits.** In other words, we mustn't limit ourselves.
- **And more importantly, don't let others' limiting beliefs hold us back.**
- **Not everyone is going to be on board from the beginning (or at all).** We may need to break away from social expectations along the way. That's fine. They are social constructs that were created by and accepted by people; they can be torn down and reconstructed in a way that better suits us.
- **Don't be surprised by those who offer support.** Accept it. Embrace it. We'll need it. Also, don't be afraid to make the call to these unlikely and unexpected supporters.
- **Don't apologize to those who expect us to be, or do, something else.** It's our life to live, not theirs.

- **Sometimes others will try to make us pay for their discomfort.** Let's own our part, but not take on theirs.
- **Persist through the discomfort.** Forging a new path and taking on new challenges is not always comfortable, but it will be worth it.
- **Not everything will go as planned.** Make the best of it, and look for new opportunities to learn and grow along the way. Learning something new often leads to new opportunities. If we end up at a dead end, we can make a new plan.
- **We can surround ourselves with people who believe in us and help us on our journey.** We don't need to go it alone. It's always good to have pals along the way. We can and should ask for help when we need it.
- **Let go of what no longer serves us.**
- **It's okay to let go of those people who refuse to see us in our new light.** Hopefully, they come around, but if they don't, don't lose hope. We'll meet new people along the way who can see us differently. People come into our lives for different reasons and don't always stay for the entire journey.
- **Be patient.** Change takes time. You've heard of overnight successes . . . most of the *overnights* were years in the making. But don't lose hope. If success takes time, it really gets absorbed into who we are and how we operate.
- **We owe it to the world to be all that we can be.** Don't hold back. Don't shrink. Be bold.

CHAPTER 2

YOU ARE HERE

It wasn't until my late forties that I started to find my footing again. I'd been feeling off-balance, and I wasn't happy. I felt as if something was missing. "Is this it?" I'd ask. "Is this all there is?"

I felt guilty about feeling this way. We were financially secure, healthy, able to enjoy life, and yet, something wasn't quite right. I considered myself professionally successful; I flew helicopters as a hobby, played tennis, had two great kids and one great husband, and had lots of good friends.

What more could I ask for?

Why was I looking for more?

Would I ever be satisfied?

Turns out that I wasn't alone in feeling this way. The midlife crisis may be a myth, but we definitely experience psychological and physiological shifts in our forties and fifties. Some of us may feel dissatisfied, restless, confused, scared, and generally unhappy. This emotional miasma often seems irrational.

Whether we can see it or not, we have a lot going on in our bodies and our minds. Hormone and brain changes. General aging. Some have even coined the phrase *midlife adolescence.*

Oh, God, I thought the first time I read that. *Not again! Wasn't one puberty enough?*

Apparently not.

Just as adolescence prepared our bodies and minds for adulthood, midlife adolescence (or midlife puberty) prepares us for the next half of our lives. Here's the really important part: the feelings are normal.

There's nothing wrong with us.

Where we are and what we are experiencing should be normalized, not stigmatized. In some cases, it should be celebrated. Midlife is considered a significant transition period, and discomfort is to be expected.

In fact, a decline in happiness is *normal.* Jonathan Rauch, author of *Happiness Curve*, says, "It's perfectly natural to feel dissatisfaction without having anything to be dissatisfied about."

I really wish someone had told me that it was okay, even normal, to be dissatisfied or unhappy before I started midlife! The happiness curve that Rauch speaks about is validating, but has been so unnerving. I'd always been a fairly happy and optimistic person, until I wasn't. I thought it was my new normal.

Rauch goes on to say, "The downturn (in happiness) is gradual, gentle but cumulative, and it sinks into a trough and is a result of growing disappointment and declining optimism."

What does one do about this?

Rauch suggests that we acknowledge it, accept it, and recognize that the decline in happiness isn't permanent. He encourages normalizing the experience and says, "Normalization helps reduce the feelings of shame and isolation. Normalizing it can help interrupt the negative feedback loop that gives midlife discontent its peculiar ability to amplify itself."

What does that mean for women in midlife?

Where you are is where you are. No judgment. No shame. No comparisons. Once we accept this, we can take our next step without hesitation. We can affix the *You Are Here* sticker on our Life board and move on.

IS THIS ALL THERE IS?

Reverend Connie Habash is a marriage and family counselor, psychotherapist, and yoga teacher based in the San Francisco Bay Area. She wrote *Awakening from Anxiety: A Spiritual Guide to Living a More Calm, Confident, and Courageous Life.* Rev. Habash works with a lot of people, especially in Silicon Valley, who are asking, "Is this all there is?" She said to me, "They've reached their goals, but find they still aren't feeling the happiness they expected. They are having what I call a *midlife awakening.*"

My cousin Casey and I had an interesting text message exchange about this very topic. She was considering looking for a new job and texted me, *I feel guilty looking for something for myself, but I feel like I've pinnacled and wonder what the next level is going to be. I don't see a clear path. At the same time, I feel like an imposter. What if I don't like what I find next?*

My response?

You are not an imposter, and there is nothing wrong with wanting more or something different. If it isn't working for you, find something different. You owe it to yourself to do so. You owe it to the world as well. Think of what you are depriving the world of as you stay in something that isn't meeting your needs and satisfying your desires. As for what if it isn't better, *you can always change your mind. Treat it as exploration. If it doesn't work out (and chances are it will to some extent), then you learn from it, take the info, and move on to the next thing to explore. It's all about exploration.*

Her perfect response came next. *That's always my approach—figure it out, learn from it, and move on if it's not working. Good input/advice. The hard part for me is talking myself out of my 'what if's.'*

Last I heard, Casey is still trying to figure it out. But our exchange helped her give herself permission—and confidence—to explore her options. I am absolutely confident she will figure it out. (She has a Ph.D. in Fire Science and is a total badass, so I'm pretty sure she can figure anything out.)

Julie Gordon White, a San Francisco Bay Area business coach, works with women who are tired of not being valued and having others control their lives and their schedules. Some of the work she's done has been with women in their forties and fifties.

"Women in their forties want to actualize," she said, "and realize that they can't *not* do it. If they haven't made the move by the time they're in their fifties, they realize that they *really* can't *not* do it. They end up doing the work and making the leap."

Between hormonal changes, brain changes, and experience, it's perfectly normal for us to feel compelled to change things up and make it more about us and less about what is *expected* of us.

It's nature's way of saying, "It's your time. Make the most of it!"

MIDLIFE TRIGGERS

The general discontentment and malaise of midlife hit me hard when I was forty-five. There was no major life event; it was more like an accumulation of smaller things.

Women are often triggered to examine their lives and make big changes when there are events such as the death of a loved one, empty-nest syndrome, serious illness, loss of a job, divorce, or some combination of these things. Some of the women I interviewed experienced one or more of these.

Here are a few of their stories.

BODY SHUTDOWN

Charlotte had it all figured out.

Or so she thought.

Her business was successful. She loved her son and her husband. Her marriage had hit a rocky patch, so they'd begun to see a therapist.

She was forty, worked from home when she wasn't traveling, and felt like she effectively balanced motherhood with being a CEO. Her son traveled with her, and she was proud of the fact that he had never been in daycare.

"During therapy," she told me, "I realized my son was the same age I was when my mother died. This discovery brought up all sorts of repressed feelings. I started asking a lot of questions about what

I was doing, why I was doing it, and whether I was doing the right things. I started making changes at work and stopped traveling as much. I put restorative time on my calendar and thought I had it under control."

She came down with pneumonia, and her doctor asked what else was going on. She said, "He was surprised I was there. It wasn't normal for someone like me, who was in good health, to get pneumonia. My body was signaling that all was not well. Apparently, my body was under significant stress, and I didn't even know it."

She scheduled more time for therapy and restorative activities. "I changed my personal and professional objectives. I stepped back, assessed where I was, and did the work required to move forward healthier and better informed."

She might have skipped a turn—but she wasn't out of the game. Now she's playing by her own rules.

Broken Heart

Leila had three close friends and family members die in rapid succession when she was forty-five. All three had been healthy when they died suddenly and unexpectedly. She was with the third one when they died.

That's when she realized she wanted out of her marriage.

While in the ICU, she called her then-husband and told him she wanted a divorce. When she returned home, she packed up and left, but returned within a year. Her daughter didn't understand why she returned. Leila said, "It was as if I were a monkey in a cage with the door open, but who refused to leave. It took four more years for me to leave my husband for good. Even though I knew it was the right thing, it wasn't until I was on a trip, became ill, and had to have angioplasty that I decided to take action."

During the angioplasty procedure, she "knew what was going on." She realized that she had forgotten to take care of her heart. During our conversation, she said, "This is one of the universe's greatest gifts to me. Now, I take better care of myself."

Her buoyant energy usually helps her live life to the fullest, but her heart surgery was the dramatic wake-up call she needed to stop pushing herself beyond her limits.

LOOKING FOR MEANING

Leila wasn't the only one who was forced to reconsider her life's purpose when illness struck. For Greta, her back taught her what she needed to know. Due to a genetic condition, she underwent a series of surgeries at the age of forty-two.

At the time, Greta had a successful corporate job and valued her independence. She'd never been married and had no kids. After the surgeries, she started asking questions. "What am I doing?" she asked. "And *why* am I doing it?"

She was looking for meaning, any meaning, and wasn't finding it in her current work.

"I experienced significant pain during the surgeries," she said. "It made me question the value of life and what I was giving my life to. After each surgery, I went back to work within a few days. I enjoyed my work but realized I wanted to have greater impact. I wanted to leave a legacy."

She quit her job, moved across the country, found a way to live cost-effectively, and decided to start a company to help others in need.

"The startup game has been tough," she said, "but I love almost every minute of it. I love knowing I am leaving the world a better place."

DEATH STORY

Unhappy in her forties, Carla had been successful in her technical position at a large corporation but didn't feel personally fulfilled.

"I didn't feel like I was getting the recognition and compensation I deserved. I watched the men around me get promoted and receive better compensation packages. For a while, I hung on to the false hope that I, too, would eventually get promoted. That it might end up being OK."

Carla isn't a big risk-taker. She knew she wanted to make a change, but she also wanted to move forward and up. "I'd worked hard to get to where I was," she said. "I didn't want to have to rebuild."

Losing her dad kicked her into a different mode—she began reflecting on her life, her high stress levels, and her heavy travel schedule. She decided she didn't want it anymore.

"Up until this point," she told me, "my job search had been deliberate. Then I hit a point where I just wanted out. A company I'd looked at a few years before offered me a job. I liked them and decided the 30% pay cut was worth it. I wanted a better quality of life, which was more important than the money."

Regardless of who you are, midlife is a time of triggers and changes. When we let it, change can spur us on to greater things and bigger places—but even listening to the triggers and finding something better for our lives isn't always enough.

LOOKING FOR MORE

In an essay in *On Being 40(ish)*, author Katie Bolick writes, "Forty-five to forty-six tends to be the nadir of women's self-reported happiness."

Most of us don't know that being at our lowest on the happiness scale is really a *thing*. I certainly didn't know it. I struggled with sifting through questions like: *Is this ambition or discontent? Do I want more because I'm ambitious or because I want to find a way to have greater impact in my life and in the world?*

The answers were surprisingly difficult to tease out.

At forty-five, I started asking questions out loud regarding my professional situation. I talked with my friends, colleagues, and pretty much anyone who would listen as I researched and worked through the angst.

I wanted my work to matter. Battling the arrogance of science in a space that didn't appreciate my whole value proposition left me feeling frustrated and exhausted. The same weary battles arose with each client on each project. It felt like I swam against the current—and ended up going nowhere.

Come to find out, I'd been asking some of the typical midlife questions, like: *How can what I do have greater meaning? How can I use my experience and knowledge to have greater impact? Is this all there is? Is this my new normal?*

It's good to be asking questions in midlife. We should be challenging our own status quo, perhaps moving out of complacency. As we ask questions, we can try to find the source of our unrest or discontent.

I started by asking questions in my professional life, but I didn't stop there. I began to question many things in my life, and continue to do so. To design the life of our own choosing, we must get a better sense of who we are, who we want to be, what we want, where we are, and what constraints we are truly living under.

ACCEPTANCE

Sometimes there are things we cannot change or things we cannot change right now.

Bill Burnett and Dave Evans said in *Designing Your Life*, "When you accept it, you are free to work around that situation and find something that is actionable."

Once we find acceptance, we can focus less on what we *can't* change and more on what we *can*. Then we can take action. It's much less frustrating and much more effective. You can begin (as they say in the book), "Taking stock of your situation, by taking your own inventory and making an assessment."

They suggest we assess our health, work, play, and love to determine what we have, don't have, or have done. The assessment of our resources, skills, experience, gaps, and needs gives us a starting point, like on a map at a mall with an arrow pointing to *You Are Here*.

Once you know where you are and where you want to go, you can begin to navigate your life path. (And if you have no clue about that, keep reading!)

YOU ARE WHERE YOU ARE

I really wish I had known in my early forties what I know now. I would have suffered a lot less doubt, angst, and shame. So many times, I found myself saying, "I'm unhappy," followed by, "but I'm so grateful for what I have and where I am." I felt terrible that my problem appeared to be a first-world, bougie problem.

We are where we are.

Until we acknowledge that what we are feeling is real and valid, it's incredibly challenging to determine our next steps.

You are absolved of all guilt associated with wanting more, feeling unhappy, or feeling any discontent regardless of the trigger or lack thereof. It's as normal as being an angsty teenager. In our forties and fifties, we're simply angsty *midlifers* with more experience and miles behind us.

Welcome to midlife.

You are here.

TAKING THE CONTROLS

— Am I where I want to be?
— In health, work, play, and love:
  • What do I have?
  • What have I done?
  • What do I need?

BRIEFING NOTES

CHAPTER 3

FINDING YOUR NEW WHY

On New Year's Eve, I slipped into our local Barnes and Noble to scope out books on midlife.

This had been on my to-do list for the better part of December, and I finally took the time to do it. I wanted to better understand the competition, get ideas for the cover, and pick up a few books to read.

In the self-help section, I browsed titles, snapped pictures of covers, and started a pile of books to buy. A wide variety from well-known authors like Brené Brown and writer/producer Shonda Rhimes found their way into my stack. Books in all sizes and colors began to pile up.

Initially, I overlooked a book called *Ikigai: The Japanese Secret to a Long and Happy Life.* I didn't think it was what I was looking for. As I continued to skim the shelves, picking up books and opening them one by one, I decided to snap a picture of the cover. My eyes kept coming back to it, so I decided to add it to the stack of books to be purchased.

I didn't have much in the way of expectations around the book. Really, how can one book have *the* secret to being happy?

During a rainy day, I hid inside and read the book in one sitting. With a bright marker, I highlighted nuggets of wisdom as I went along. There was so much goodness in the book that as soon as I was done, I handed it to my husband. He had been struggling with finding his purpose (his *ikigai*). "Read this. Now," I said. "And ignore my highlights." He laughed and, uncharacteristically, started reading the book.

So—what is our *ikigai*? According to this book, it's the reason we get up in the morning. Why is it important? "When we spend our days feeling connected to what is meaningful to us, we live more fully; when we lose the connection, we feel despair," it says.

During midlife, a lot of us (men and women), lose sight of our purpose. That makes the rest of our lives wobbly. Our health and happiness depend on strong friendships, a little exercise, and waking up each day with a strong sense of purpose.

But how do we find that meaning and purpose?

How do we find our *why*?

WHAT IS YOUR WHY?

Some people wake up one day in their forties and start questioning everything. For others, it's a gradual slide until you wonder *what the hell happened?* Then there are some who never experience the need to question what they're meant to do.

Susanne Biro, Executive Coach to executive-level leaders based in Vancouver, spoke with me about midlife. She is a delightfully perceptive, optimistic, and encouraging person.

In one of our conversations, she said, "It's not unusual for my clients to ask questions like, *'Is this all there is?'* when we begin our work together. It makes sense that we start to question the fact that, as much as we obtain out there, it often does little to change what we care most about, which is how we feel inside. Many of us are starting to sense the roadmap we've been following is flawed, and there must be another way to experience ourselves and others in the world."

"Are all of your clients asking these types of questions?" I asked.

"No," she said. "For some people, this doesn't occur. But for many, there is a growing awareness that they really seek greater peace, joy, fulfillment, and that nothing outside of them has ever brought it for very long. This is an incredible time of creation. But it also requires a level of maturation to ask, *'Where is my sense of self?'*"

Susanne said that she "wishes that all people would listen to and live their own truth more than they do. Then, when the world sings their praises, or tears them down, neither matter. When we are self-defined and living our own truth, neither matters."

Of course, there's no right way to find your *why*, but I do have some suggestions to get you started, taken from the article, "Do You Know Your Why?"[2]

1. Identify what makes you come alive. It's usually connected to a cause bigger than you.
2. Add in the things you've always been good at. Figure out how you can apply your skills, knowledge, and experience to add the most value.
3. Decide how you want to measure your life.

Your *why* is at the intersection of these three.

There's no rule that says that once you define your *why*, you can't change it. The important thing is to do the work to find it and periodically reassess to ensure you still have it.

Margie Warrell put it beautifully when she said, "Only when you know your *why* will you find the courage to take the risks needed to get ahead, stay motivated when the chips are down, and move your life onto an entirely new, more challenging, and rewarding trajectory."

Knowing your *why* helps you truly thrive in life.

Designing Your Life

That day at Barnes and Noble turned out to be expensive. I bought no fewer than ten books on midlife. One of them was the previously mentioned *Designing Your Life* by Stanford educators Bill Burnett and Dave Evans. For anyone looking to find their purpose, whether in life or in their careers, this is a must-read.

Why did I love it?

They took the basic questions about meaning and purpose and reframed the search for answers using design thinking. Design thinking is a creative problem-solving approach that relies on empathy, ideation, and experimentation. In other words, brainstorm a bunch of ideas, start playing with them, enlist the aid of others, and figure out what works for you.

Easy peasy!

If we look at midlife as a time of exploration and let go of the end goal, we never know what might show up. It's a time to play, be curious, experiment, and see what happens. It means getting uncomfortable (but really, if you're in midlife, you're already uncomfortable!) and letting go of expectations. The process never ends, which means you keep playing and experimenting, and there's really no *getting it right*. It just is.

One of my favorite lines in the book says, "There are many versions of you, and they are all right." I love this freedom—we don't have to be boxed into a category.

Using this method, life design boils down to the following:

- Be curious
- Try stuff
- Reframe problems
- Know it's a process
- Ask for help

As for experimentation and exploration, hang tight. We'll talk more about that later in the book.

GETTING OUTSIDE YOUR COMFORT ZONE

Ann was fifty-one when she began searching for her midlife purpose. She started working with a personal brand strategist and hired an executive coach. "I should have done it years ago," she said.

One January, she found herself at a Parlay House event in San Francisco. The event featured a panel of four women discussing the topic of midlife renewal. All of them had taken part in Julia Cameron's twelve-week program *The Artist's Way*, designed to help artists and non-artists discover or reclaim their creativity.

Desperately seeking her own renewal in midlife, Ann was inspired by these women's stories to give Julia's program a shot. "Starting a program like *The Artist's Way* was completely out of character for me," she admitted to me, "but I felt that I had to do something radically different in order to get clarity on the next chapter of my life. I ordered the book the next day and jumped in."

Part of the program is called *the morning pages,* which are three handwritten pages done every morning that act like a mental palate cleanser. Of these, Ann said, "Initially, I dreaded the daily morning pages. I had never kept a journal before and done that level of excavation about my feelings, desires, and fears. But then, I started to look forward to them. They truly help you unload years of mental baggage. Baggage you don't even realize you're carrying. Writing the pages gives you extraordinary clarity about what you want or don't want. It helps you confront fears that are holding you back. The exercise can be a game changer if you let it. I became a believer and have encouraged many other women to do it."

This was just the beginning for Ann to find her greater purpose. She continued to work with the people she calls "Team Ann." She encourages every woman to assemble her team—people who are supporting her, advising her, and cheering her on. Through this deep discovery work, she gained the courage to be the CEO of her own company after always being comfortable as the second-in-command. She found something she was passionate about and launched the company.

We can safely say she has found her *why.* She wakes up each morning determined to make a difference in the world through the mission of her company.

LOOKING TO GOD FOR ANSWERS

Amy was in her mid-thirties when she started asking herself about her purpose in life.

She had checked all the right boxes. College. CPA. MBA.

Marriage. Nice car. Nice house. Solid career. Yet . . . she wasn't happy. *Why not?* she asked herself. *What have I been doing wrong?*

"I started questioning whether I had been focused on the right things in life," she said. "My midlife crisis resulted in a divorce. I felt lost, turned to theology, and ended up becoming a born-again Christian. As my faith grew, I felt more confident that my volunteer work would have a positive impact in God's kingdom."

She went on to say, "Seven years later, I was an angel investor and became involved in the entrepreneurial community. I felt unsure whether my investments truly fell within what God intended for me, and I began to question whether I was doing the right thing. After much soul-searching, I realized the answers were within the New Testament in the Parable of the Talents, where faithfulness and stewardship were demonstrated through wise investments in alignment with one's ability."

She ended by saying, "Through Bible study, I understand that God has a plan for everyone, including me, and I no longer worry about it. Every day I choose to be happy and contribute to my community through investing and volunteer work."

BE INTENTIONAL

Barbara Bradley Hagerty, author of *Life Reimagined,* says, "Midlife is a time to recalibrate, not surrender."

If you've been living your life on autopilot, now is the time to reengage and find your soul's purpose. In her book, she argues, "Pursuing passions and hobbies is not incidental. It can hone your brain; it can boost your health. It can save your life."

If you're feeling less than fulfilled and find yourself asking, "Is this all there is?" you can take the controls and find greater meaning and purpose in your life. Of course, this doesn't mean you have to give away everything you own and surrender your life to some purpose (unless that's what you really want to do).

This is a great time to take inventory of your life and assess where you are. Be honest about what is working and what isn't, what is fulfilling and what isn't, what gives you energy versus what drains your energy. Take your obligations into account, of course, but at the same time, be honest and generous when considering your own needs.

Barbara says, "Part of midlife's challenge is to closely examine the old script, the one that family and society writes for you, the one in which you are meeting everyone else's expectations, and see if it needs revision. The new script is tailored to your core identity, your own talents, passions, and personality, and these shape your goals."

And with your goals—your meaning and purpose.

WE WANT TO MATTER

We want our lives to have been worthwhile; all of us want to *matter*. We want to know that we left the world a better place.

Executive coach Susanne Biro said, "You don't have to move to another country to make a difference. You can choose to do something every day to make a positive impact with the people right in front of you. Start at home, start at the coffee shop, the airport . . ."

I haven't given my legacy much thought, but I am starting to. Legacy feels like something that old people with a lot of money are concerned about. Then again, I used to think fifty-five was old. Not anymore.

As we reimagine how we want to be in the world, we can look forward to what we want while we are here. And then, we can imagine ourselves looking back to see what we want to have left behind. To create our new *why*, we can merge the two.

With that desire to have an impact and leave a legacy comes the passion and desire to get out of bed and do something with meaning and purpose. This is our *ikigai*.

COURSE CORRECTIONS

As a project manager, I plan projects. I joke with my clients that as soon as the project plan is created, it is obsolete. In a perfect world, with perfect team members and perfect resources, everything can go according to plan. I live in reality, not PerfectionLand, and I regularly adjust and re-plan to make sure the project stays on target. I also have to regularly confirm that our target is still valid. Sometimes, requirements change. That means the project changes—or even ends—before it's complete.

The same holds true when I fly. It's not uncommon to get a weather briefing and mentally plan my flight path, only to change my plan while in flight. San Francisco air traffic control may not let me fly through their airspace, or San Francisco may be fogged in. So, I will change course and head toward Napa or San Jose. I change my destination to accommodate for factors outside of my control.

A few years ago, I flew my husband and daughter to Monterey for lunch. On the way back, the weather had deteriorated on our planned flight path, and we had to head up the coast instead of straight inland. We continued to head back toward our home airport but had to fly an extra thirty miles to skirt the weather. My objective remained the same, but I had to change the path to my destination.

Like with flying and projects, once you've set your course to your new *why*, you will have to monitor and adjust. You may have to correct for external and internal factors. You may decide to set a new course altogether. But having a general sense of where you want to go makes it easier to withstand and overcome obstacles you encounter on your journey.

This is an ongoing process that requires vigilance and intention.

TAKING THE CONTROLS

— What is my *ikigai*?
— What do I want my legacy to be?
— Am I living my soul's purpose?

BRIEFING NOTES

....
....
....
....
....
....
....
....
....
....
....
....
....
....
....
....
....
....
....
....
....
....

TOP 10 MIDLIFE SUGGESTIONS FROM DESIGNING YOUR LIFE

My husband has been a David Letterman fan since he was old enough to watch his late-night show. (I often describe my husband as a cross between Doogie Howser, David Letterman, and Steve Martin.) When we moved in together in our mid-twenties and still had cable, I would try to stay up to watch with him. While I didn't watch often, I did enjoy the show's Top 10 segment. It's a great vehicle for sharing lists, so thank you, Mr. Letterman!

The following is a list of my Top 10 favorite midlife suggestions from the book *Designing Your Life*.

10. Keep your intimates informed.
9. Life design gives you endless mulligans (do-overs).
8. Log your failures.
7. Once you make your choice, embrace your choice, and go for it.
6. Take the slow path of prototyping first.
5. Follow the joy. Follow what engages and excites you, what brings you alive.
4. Do not fall in love with your first idea.
3. There are lots of different paths you could take to live each of those productive, amazingly different lives.
2. Embrace being stuck.

And the number-one thing to remember is . . .

1. **Life design is a journey; let go of the end goal.**

Chapter 4

HEALTH CHECK: MENOPAUSE AND GENERAL HEALTH

Every eighteen months, I go in for my annual gynecological exam. It's not a fun process. I really hate picking up the phone to schedule an appointment three to four weeks out, and I really hate having to block out four hours (including drive time) for a fifteen-minute appointment. I may show up on time, but because of the way the doctors have to schedule their time, they are invariably late for appointments.

Then there's the actual appointment, with the paper bolero jackets that don't cover your boobs and a huge, crinkly paper towel that barely covers your lower half and your bare ass, which is sweating and sticking to the paper.

Last time I went, I sat in the exam room half naked, trying not to look at the tools laid out on the tray. I'd already run the gauntlet of the annual weighing like a farm animal at a 4-H competition, not to mention questions about my last period. I fidgeted, wondering when the doctor would come in. Would it be two minutes or twenty? There should be an app that gives us an estimated wait time and a place to put questions. White Coat Syndrome is real! Whenever the doctor comes into the room, I always lose my ability to think clearly.

The minutes tick by as my naked butt is getting stickier, and I get even more uncomfortable. At this point, it's inevitable that the paper will rip when I have to scooch my butt closer to the stirrups. You know the drill.

Finally, the doctor walks in. While reviewing her notes, she glances up and says the thing I've been dreading, "You've gained weight, Terri."

No shit.

She asks about my eating (and drinking) habits and suggests that I *do something about it.*

"Uh, ok," I say. "I know. Thanks."

Then we move into the second-most unpleasant part of the appointment without any discussion about midlife health changes.

The experience with my primary care physician (PCP) was similar, without the vaginal probing, thankfully. During my last appointment, my PCP asked, "Can you make some dietary changes to lose weight?"

"I can," I said. "The question is, will I?"

That pretty much shut him up.

None of my healthcare providers said anything about how perimenopause makes it nearly impossible for women to lose weight. What if one of them told me this five to seven years ago? Then I could have made it a priority to maintain a lower number on the scale (after actually purchasing a scale).

Why don't doctors talk to us about menopause and give us a heads-up? Why are perimenopause, menopause, and postmenopause grouped under menopause? At my annual exams, other than the regularity of my periods, my doctors never mentioned menopause, what to expect, or health risk factors.

We don't need to be scolded.

We need to be *educated.*

Between hormone changes, sleep changes, and metabolic changes, the weight gain and weight shift become inevitable. I haven't yet hit the night sweat stage (or at least not that I am aware of—although I do wake up a little stinkier than I used to) or the hot flash stage, but I've definitely seen an increase in facial hair. And then there's the weight thing.

Every once in a while, I have trouble remembering a word or a name, or I lose track of my own train of thought. I thought I was drinking too much and then realized that it was the brain fog of perimenopause. I learned about these things when I was forty-eight.

It would have been nice to have someone explain this to me at forty-one. Or better yet, at thirty-nine.

There are books on menopause that attempt to cover, in hundreds of pages, the myriad of things that crop up around health in midlife. I am not trying to replicate what is covered in those books, but I do want to raise awareness around the things that aren't spoken of and begin to normalize the conversations around what to expect before you get there. Or, if you are already there, to let you know you aren't crazy.

Let's start with menopause.

THE MYSTERY OF MENOPAUSE

In my early and mid-forties, I thought I was too young for menopause, and it was something to worry about later. My assumption was that menopause was for women over the age of fifty, which clearly wasn't me.

To get us all on the same page, here are a few important definitions:

Perimenopause: the transitional time before menopause and postmenopause. It's also referred to as the *menopause transition.*

Menopause: the point in time at which you've gone twelve months without a period, unrelated to pregnancy or other biological/ physiological conditions.

Postmenopause: the time after menopause (sometimes synonymous with menopause).

It turns out that menopause isn't just a fifties thing; it can start much earlier.

I didn't even know what perimenopause was until I started talking to a founder focused on menopause when we were working on her investor presentation. This was well into what was most likely my menopause transition.

Why did I have to learn about my body by working with a founder? And why is menopause such a mystery?

Talking about menopause often feels embarrassing and shameful. Why is that? Even now, I whisper the words or say them behind a cupped hand. Why should a normal human phase be considered a taboo topic?

The simple answer is that we're youth-obsessed in the U.S. and see aging as a disease. Our society doesn't value women, either.

All of these things need to—and will—change. Of this, I am absolutely certain.

THIRTY-FOUR SYMPTOMS OF MENOPAUSE? WAIT . . . WHAT?

Despite extensive research, there are still so many questions about menopause that remain unanswered for most women.

Here is a small sampling:

1. How will I know if I have started the menopause transition?
2. Are there obvious signs?
3. How long will it last for me?
4. What types of symptoms can I expect?
5. What treatments are available?
6. Should I consider hormone replacement therapy?
7. What should I be paying attention to now?

Unfortunately, the answers depend on our family history, our biology, our environment, our stressors, and our lifestyle. It also depends on whether you are a person of color or white. If you're a person of color, you may reach menopause two years earlier than white women, who reach it, on average, at fifty-one-and-a-half years of age.

Dr. Arline Geronimus from the University of Michigan School of Public Health says, "The accumulation of toxic stress, largely due to a lifetime of constant racial-based discrimination and aggression, micro and overt, literally deteriorates the bodies of black women."[3]

This may make for longer, hotter, and more extreme menopause transitions. If you're a black woman, you're more likely to enter perimenopause earlier and are at greater risk of health conditions like loss of bone density and cardiovascular disease. According to Dr. Geronimus, the good news is that you're at a lower risk for breast, endometrial, and ovarian cancers.

While researching menopause, I stumbled on a list of the symptoms of menopause. I'd heard about the number before but didn't read the list until I prepared for this book.

And holy shit!

The common symptoms like hot flashes, night sweats, weight gain, loss of libido, vaginal dryness, mood swings, insomnia, sleep disorders, incontinence, and irregular periods are fairly well known.

Mother nature is a bitch.

But some of the others are slightly crazy. Burning tongue? Tingling extremities? Electric shock sensation? When I read that one, I thought that was the treatment!

What are the others, you might ask? Here we go:

1. Memory lapses
2. Fatigue
3. UTIs
4. Bloating
5. Hair loss/thinning
6. Dizziness
7. Headaches
8. Digestive problems
9. Muscle tension
10. Allergies
11. Brittle nails

12. Change in body odor
13. Itchy skin
14. Difficulty concentrating
15. Irregular heartbeat
16. Anxiety
17. Depression
18. Joint pain
19. Breast pain (I had breast pain about six months ago and thought I had breast cancer because I had no idea this was a symptom of perimenopause. I definitely had some stress and anxiety worrying about that one!)

One symptom I didn't list was panic disorder because of conflicting information.

There's just not enough understood about women at this stage of our lives (or any stage of our lives) to get a truly definitive list of symptoms. And there's not enough known to provide us with concrete answers as to what will happen to us in menopause, why it happens to us, and the best way to treat these symptoms.

That's why it's so important to pay attention, seek out knowledgeable healthcare professionals, and take care of ourselves.

HARNESSING THE POWER OF MIDLIFE TO CHANGE THE WORLD

Women in midlife constantly impress me. None of us are ready to be turned out to pasture, and all of us need to recognize that *this is our time*. Several women said they were just hitting their stride and feeling like they were at the top of their game.

Thanks to midlife, we have a huge opportunity to harness this energy and power. With that power, we can drive change without losing sight of what we need as women. Imagine if we all claimed this power. What if we stopped seeing menopause as an ugly and shameful word or time?

That's why health in midlife takes center stage. If we better understand our bodies, our changing minds, how to take care of ourselves, and the crucial imperative to make our health a priority, we could change the world.

GOING-OUT-OF-BUSINESS SALE

On top of all the menopause symptoms, there's the *going-out-of-business sale* that is our body's signal to get busy if we want to contribute to the world's population. Our hormones increase and let us know that now is the time for us to have our last baby (or babies) if we are so inclined.

My sex drive went through the roof, and I nearly ruined my marriage with my desire for more and better sex. It would have been nice to know that this was a *thing* and would last about a year before settling back into a more normal pattern.

MAKING YOUR HEALTH YOUR PRIORITY

As women in midlife, we will most likely experience hormonal changes that compel us to look inward and focus on ourselves. We've been taking care of others for decades. Now is the time to *mother* ourselves.

Not too surprisingly, many experts say that midlife is the time to take better care of ourselves—physically and mentally—in order to thrive and set ourselves up for a positive *later in life*. Barbara Bradley Hagerty talks about this in detail in *Life Reimagined*.

If we don't take good care of ourselves in midlife and fail to manage our symptoms and health during the menopause transition, we can create additional, more tenacious health issues. Metabolic disease. Heart disease. Osteoporosis. And other chronic conditions that can be mitigated or avoided altogether. *Enduring* in midlife doesn't lead to better mental and physical health.

More campaigns have been raising awareness around women and heart disease, but most of us seem more afraid of cancer than cardio-vascular issues. Dr. Sarah Speck, a Seattle-based cardiologist, said, "At the age of forty-five, one in nine women will have some form of heart disease, and by the age of sixty-five, this will increase to one in three."[4]

Unless referred to a cardiologist by our primary care doctors, most of us aren't aware of potential risk factors based on our health history. We need holistic care across our entire lives, rather than at a single point in time.

In the same article, Dr. Speck outlined the following risk factors:

- Studies in 2018 showed that women who experienced hypertension or preeclampsia during pregnancy are four to six times more likely to develop hypertension later in life.
- They also have a 70% increased risk of type 2 diabetes and have signs of heart disease earlier in life than women without hypertension during pregnancy.
- Women with gestational diabetes are more likely to develop diabetes and hypertension decades after pregnancy and so increase their individual risk of heart disease or stroke.
- Postpartum depression or menopause-related depression can increase a woman's risk for heart disease, as can radiation treatment associated with breast cancer.

Dr. Speck says, "Recognizing risk factors is an opportunity to use your lifestyle choices to prevent you from having a heart attack or stroke."

And then there's Alzheimer's.

Dr. Hemalee Patel, a San Francisco-based, board-certified internal medicine doctor reports a possible connection between heart health and Alzheimer's risk.[5] She says, "Alzheimer's and heart disease share several similar risk factors like obesity, diabetes, and high cholesterol." Dr. Patel recommends exercise, a high-quality diet (whole food, plant-based, healthy unsaturated fats, quality protein, antioxidants), getting adequate sleep, and creating new neural pathways by learning new things.

Dr. Carliza Marcos, a dentist out of San Carlos, California, also says we can't forget about our teeth and gums. Just as adolescents have issues with gingivitis due to hormonal changes, midlife women experience periodontal disease (gum disease) because of hormonal changes too. That reminds me; I am due for a cleaning and should probably start flossing.

If we don't start taking care of our health in midlife, we risk significant health challenges later. Midlife is time for our ounce of prevention.

MENTAL HEALTH AND ISOLATION

Despite blaming the rainy weather for keeping me inside all winter, while reading a few articles, I realized that I had gone into hiding.

Isolation is a common phenomenon for women in the perimenopause/menopause transition.[6] This could stem from irritability, anxiety, depression, fatigue, loss of social circles due to divorce, and embarrassment from hair loss, weight gain, or body odor, among other things.

For me, a combination of things contributed to it. Primarily my weight gain. I didn't feel good in my own body; I was embarrassed by what others might think was a lack of self-control, and my clothes didn't fit well. Staying home was far easier than attempting to muster the energy to get out . . . but, getting out was exactly what I needed.

Based on my research, spending time with people may be the best remedy.

The more I talk to other women, the more I realize that I'm not alone. Unless I get out and speak with other women, I think I'm the only one, and the cycle of isolation continues. We need to talk about aging, menopause, and other things like stress incontinence, increased anxiety, and vaginal dryness. Let's normalize these topics and remove the guilt and shame.

Even as I bought a few books on menopause, I felt slightly embarrassed, kind of like when I've purchased tampons. If we get out of our isolation and start talking about these things, we can desensitize ourselves and remove the perceived stigmas.

We can't do this in isolation.

BEYOND SOCIAL ANXIETY

Because we stopped having children by the time I started perimenopause, and I chose to have a procedure to deal with heavy menstrual bleeding (a fairly common perimenopausal issue) in my mid-forties, I don't feel a sense of loss around the end of the reproductive stage of my life.

When I stopped breastfeeding my second child and we decided to be happy with two, I came to terms with it quickly. However, some women experience anxiety and possibly depression when the opportunity to give birth isn't available. Other women feel relieved they don't have to worry about getting pregnant. Some women who didn't have children—whether it was their choice or not—may experience difficult feelings during the menopause transition.

As a general rule, big and difficult feelings tend to come up during this time.

It's not uncommon for women to experience increased anxiety, whether it's from loss of fertility, aging parents, empty nests, or other body changes during midlife. Apparently, all of these plus hormones and loss of sleep can lead to increased anxiety. Twenty-three percent of women experience symptoms of anxiety during perimenopause.[7]

These anxiety symptoms aren't necessarily linked to depression. *Note: see a healthcare professional if you are experiencing panic attacks. These are not typical during menopause.*

One woman I spoke with said, "I'm forty-four. I had no idea that I could be perimenopausal and that increased anxiety could be a symptom of my hormone and body changes."

Since we aren't educated on what to expect, she, like many women, assumed that anxiety was the result of juggling parenting, her job, and living her life.

I've experienced increased anxiety around closed places. I have always been claustrophobic, but over the last year or two, the feeling has heightened. When the Thai soccer team was trapped in the cave, I couldn't read about it without nausea and sweaty hands. When I tried to do the Balance Float (a sensory deprivation chamber), I panicked after the lights went out—even though I didn't close the top. My anxiety didn't calm until I climbed free and removed the earplugs. Even having the lights on, with my eyes open and the top up, I *still* had to get out.

Various treatment options for anxiety during the menopause transition exist, including lifestyle changes. Since I'm not a healthcare professional, I won't make any recommendations in this book other than to suggest you educate yourself and seek assistance from your healthcare provider.

BEYOND ANXIETY

Beyond anxiety, there is depression.

There is so much going on for women in midlife. With the resurfacing of old issues and traumas, changes in hormones, and shifts in our lives, some women experience more than mood swings and a little social anxiety.

In fact, some women experience depression for the first time. Others experience it as a recurrence of a previous depression. According to a study released by JAMA Psychiatry[8], a woman's risk of depression doubles or even quadruples during the menopause transition. The key message for women is that depression during perimenopause and early postmenopause should be taken seriously, and women at this stage of life should be more closely monitored for depressive symptoms.

Causes of depression can range from hormonal changes, personal loss, a medical condition, and/or drug and alcohol use. Women are at greater risk if they have a history of depression or family history of depression, they have had postpartum depression, they have suffered from PMS, or they have recently suffered a major loss.

Symptoms of depression in midlife are no different than at other times in a woman's life. If you think you're experiencing the symptoms of depression, get educated and seek professional help.

MIDLIFE AND YOUR BRAIN

The book *The Wisdom of Menopause* by Christiane Northrup, MD made me feel like a case right out of a textbook.

She says, "As these hormone-driven changes affect the brain, they give a woman a sharper eye for inequity and injustice, and a voice that insists on speaking up about them."

This explains so much! The last four years, I've been speaking out against injustices, looking for ways to level the playing field, and standing up for others without a voice. I've also been advocating for better healthcare for women. In many ways, I feel compelled by my power and privilege in ways that I hadn't before the age of forty-five. Even for me, this is a new level of vocal!

We may experience brain changes that can spark creativity in magnificent ways. Some women experience newfound and explosive creativity around fifty that lasts for twenty-five to thirty years.

How's that for something to look forward to?

Denise Park, a neuroscientist, said in the book *Life Reimagined*, "I think midlife is the best time of all for your brain. You've reached a stage in your life where you have both cognitive resources (speed, memory, working memory, sort of working horsepower), but at the same time, you have knowledge, experience, and judgment. Probably the most efficient, effective time of your life."

All my research echoes this sentiment—a woman's brain is on fire in midlife. Unlike hot flashes, this is a good thing!

Not all is good with our brains in midlife, and some statistics are scary for women. Approximately one in six women will develop Alzheimer's disease compared to one in eleven men, and it's not because women live longer than men—as originally presumed.[9] Research doesn't yet explain why or definitively point to the cause of Alzheimer's. Currently, there are no effective treatments, either. Our best bet is to be proactive and protect our brain health.

Dr. Hemalee Patel says, "Making healthy choices when it comes to diet, physical activity, and everyday behaviors are essential preventive measures."[10] Keeping your brain intact for as long as possible seems to be the key here; this is where resilience, spending time with other people, and having a deep sense of purpose are beneficial. These things can actually help to hold off dementia, including Alzheimer's.

Barbara Bradley Hagerty says, "Midlife presents a fork in the road: one route leads to dementia and the other to healthy aging."

We can actively protect our brains (and our overall health) by staying engaged, remaining interested in our lives, and getting regular exercise.

Is It Getting Hot in Here?

Most of the women I know started thinking about menopause when they started to experience night sweats and hot flashes.

Scant research into women's health means no one really knows what causes hot flashes. It seems to be a combination of hormones and a wonky internal thermostat.

Every woman will have her own individual experience with hot flashes and how long they last. Some won't even get them. On average, hot flashes can persist from seven to ten years. Black women on average experience hot flashes for ten years while white women experience them for six-and-a-half years. For Latinas, it's nine years.

The ultimate question always comes out: do we have to put up with them, or is there something we can do?

Without a solid understanding of their cause, treatment options vary between medical, behavioral, and holistic approaches. There is no magic pill or lifestyle change that will make these go away. Although I did speak to a fifty-five-year-old, kick-ass woman on the tennis court who said her hot flashes went away when she took estrogen.

If you're one of the 50-75% of women who experience hot flashes, do some research, talk to a trusted healthcare provider with experience in this space, ask your friends, and see what works best for you. Ten years is a long time to simply grin and bear it. You shouldn't have to. If you don't like the answers you get, push for new and better solutions.

Make some noise while you're getting all sweaty!

So Many Unknowns

In midlife, Jeanne found herself taking care of a sick family member for nearly three years. The work consumed her. It wasn't until the demands of care lessened that she discovered she was going through the menopause transition. After neglecting her own care for so long, she finally decided to take a break and care for herself by seeking some help.

She found a new gynecologist who ended up being dismissive and unhelpful. Nevertheless, she continued to ask for tests and answers. As her symptoms worsened, he only offered drugs to manage her pain.

"It was at this point that I got angry and started digging around for options that would work for me," she told me. "I discovered that the healthcare system was not only broken and fragmented, but offered very little support for women going through the menopause transition. There was little information. It was difficult to find experts, community, and research data. There was no real understanding of traditional remedies."

I share the concern that doctors don't have much training in this area, and there's not been enough clinical research to offer viable options. As my friend Jacqueline has said, "The doctors simply expect you to *ride that dragon*." That seems unacceptable, not to mention unreasonable, when you face four to twelve years (or longer) of symptoms. It's ridiculous and unnecessary, and it can lead to other health complications.

Not one to sit idly by and wait for things to get better, Jeanne did a lot of research. She found some herbs that treated her symptoms and resolved them very quickly. She thought others might benefit from her research and launched *Mighty Menopause* to expand the resource options for midlife women.

She's also working on encouraging women to talk about what they're going through, and not simply hang on. There are options. There are choices. But we need to talk about these things with our health practitioners, our friends, and our partners, and demand better diagnostic and treatment options.

And when I talk about treatment options, I am not just talking about pharmaceutical options.

TAKING ACTION

It may seem that it's all doom and gloom surrounding health in midlife, but it doesn't have to be. If we're honest with ourselves, we need to ask a few questions:

1. Am I willing to take control of my health?
2. How can I be my own advocate?

3. What lifestyle changes can I (or am I willing to) make so I can truly thrive in midlife?
4. What would this look like?

First of all, we have to acknowledge that this is where we are. We can't be ostriches, pretending that perimenopause is what happens to other women—older women—and that it won't happen to us.

Secondly, we must take a realistic assessment of our lifestyles and health conditions. We can seek out health providers who are trained to help women in midlife. We can research and better understand our bodies and what options are available. Understanding our health risks is also helpful.

The next step is to make changes that can truly make a difference over time. There is no single pathway for all women; we need to find what works for us based on our risk factors and symptoms, then put our own plan together.

For me, adding stretching, meditation, breathing, supplements, and two plant-based dinners a week is where I started. I haven't cut out alcohol, but I have cut back to fewer nights per week. I hired a nutritional therapist and committed to doing two of her detox programs each year and have adjusted my eating habits. I actively seek new activities to build neural pathways and protect my brain. The latest has been poker, learning French, and writing this book. I also hired a new doctor; we're taking a look at my genetic risk factors to see what other changes I should start putting into place.

This is not the time for us to be passive about our health.

TAKING THE CONTROLS

— Do I know my health risk factors?
— How healthy and strong do I feel?
— What am I willing to do to protect my body and my brain?

BRIEFING NOTES

YOU MIGHT BE IN
PERIMENOPAUSE IF . . .

1. You wake up in the middle of the night in a pool of sweat.
2. You strip off your clothes as quickly as possible to cool down . . . but you aren't in the sun or a sauna.
3. You have no idea when your next period is coming (or what it's going to be like). Period trackers are useless.
4. You forget what you're saying mid-sentence, and it's not because you drank too much.
5. You and your neighbor's toddler have the same attention span and—*squirrel!*
6. Your head is pounding, and it isn't the extra glass (or three) of wine you had the night before.
7. You discover extra padding around your middle and an unexplainable, tenacious, and excess amount of *everything* on your body.
8. You're competing with your man-friends for the best five o'clock shadow.
9. Your beautiful locks are a little less plentiful and aren't reacting to color treatments the way they used to.
10. Your hair isn't the only brittle thing on your body; your nails seem to want in on the dry party.
11. You are a lot less interested in getting busy in the bedroom. When you finally get going, your natural lubricant seems to have disappeared.
12. You notice some extra moisture and wetness in your panties, and it isn't because you're all hot and bothered.
13. Your mouth or tongue is on fire, even if you aren't.

14. You itch like a dog with fleas but without the insect manifestation.
15. Your moods are like the old backyard swing, but a lot less predictable.
16. You wonder when nighttime and sleep became your enemy, especially since you're tired all the time. Between the night sweats, insomnia, sleep-breathing disorders, and anxiety, you just want the night to be over already.
17. You're a bit more odiferous than you used to be. Your deodorant is not up to the task.
18. You're dizzy but aren't drunk or on a Ferris wheel.
19. You wonder what truck hit you, or if you did a triathlon in your sleep, because your body is sore and stiff.
20. You seem to be allergic to things you weren't previously allergic to, or your allergies are worse than ever despite taking your meds.
21. Your belly and digestive tract are in a full civil war against you, and it wasn't the extra-spicy buffalo wings or full-dairy ice cream.
22. You retain water like a camel.
23. Your girl parts struggle with balancing your healthy bacteria, leaving you with more UTIs than you saw in college when you were sowing your wild oats.
24. Your *hoo-ha* isn't the only thing tingling and burning. Your arms and legs have jumped onto this bandwagon, looking for some extra fun.
25. Your bones have decided to decay at an accelerated rate.
26. Your heart skips and adds beats like a bad rapper.
27. You discover new pain in your breasts and send terrified texts to your gynecologist asking if this is normal or if you should be concerned about breast cancer.

28. You're wondering if you have some new disease because your joints are equally uncomfortable.

29. Your anxiety feels like when you were underage with alcohol in your trunk and a cop staring at you.

30. You experience irrational anxiety or fear and can't seem to calm yourself down.

31. You feel sad and can't seem to shake the feeling or muster up any interest like you used to.

32. The feeling of electricity hums under your skin, and not in a good way; like a rubber band snapping between your skin and muscle.

Here's a list of symptoms associated with the menopause transition:

- Night sweats
- Hot flashes
- Irregular periods
- Memory lapses
- Difficulty concentrating
- Headaches
- Weight gain
- Unwanted hair growth
- Thinning or loss of hair
- Brittle nails
- Loss of libido
- Incontinence
- Burning tongue
- Itchy skin
- Mood swings
- Insomnia
- Fatigue
- Sleep disorders
- Change in body odor
- Dizziness
- Joint pain
- Allergies
- Digestive issues
- Water retention
- UTIs
- Tingling extremities
- Osteoporosis
- Irregular heartbeat
- Breast pain and tenderness
- Anxiety
- Panic disorder
- Depression
- Electric shocks
- And more . . .

CHAPTER 5

CREATING LIFT:
PERMISSION AND MINDSET

O ver spring break in 2019, I told the family to plan on a Forced
Family Fun day (what I call family time) to celebrate my birthday. I had exclusive access to them for a full day to do whatever I
wanted to do. And you know what?

I couldn't decide what to do.

We could drive five hours to Magic Mountain to ride roller coast-
ers all day, which would be fun for me and the kids but not my
husband. Or we could have a day at home doing puzzles while it
rained and making dinner as a family, finishing up with a delicious
dessert made by my daughter.

I struggled to answer the most basic of questions: What did I
really want?

The struggle existed because I've been trained to be more concerned about what other people want/need than what I want for
myself. My kids kept nudging me toward what I wanted. All I wanted
was to not feel disappointed by a shitty birthday.

What did we end up doing?

We got up at 4:30 a.m., were on the road by 5:00 a.m., and in the
park at Magic Mountain by 10:45 a.m. We spent all day crisscrossing the
park, taking advantage of the Flash Pass to avoid lines for the rides. By
6:00 p.m., we were filled up on funnel cake and back on the road. After
stopping for dinner in cow country, we were home by 12:29 a.m.

The next day we were all a little sore from the rides, walking
17,000 steps, and laughing so much. My heart was full, and I couldn't
have been happier. I felt prepared to embark on a new year (the last
one in my forties!).

Something happens to us biologically during midlife, that drives our need to take care of ourselves instead of everyone else. Unfortunately, we've been shaped by society to feel guilty about it.

Frankly, that's bullshit.

We can reject this social construct and create what we want. We must decide that we are deserving. And then, we must give ourselves permission to create our own version of lift and take steps toward a more meaningful, impactful, and integrated life.

Yes, you are worth it. You are deserving. You get to create your own definition of happiness, success, and fulfillment.

You get to choose *you*.

For some of us, it's easier said than done. But there's no better time than midlife to be doing it. Christiane Northrup, MD, in her book *The Wisdom of Menopause* says that for our midlife transformation to be successful, "We must be willing to take full responsibility for the problems in our lives, and then we must be willing to feel the pain of loss and grieve for the parts of our lives that we are leaving behind."

Midlife is about owning our shit, letting go of unnecessary and unhelpful shit, and then choosing what we want. It almost becomes a mantra: I deserve this. I am worthy. I want this. I give myself permission to want what I want.

This can apply to little things, like what you want for breakfast. Or something bigger. Who do you want in your life? Where do you want to live? What work do you want to do? Do you even have to work? What do you want your legacy to be?

It's all about permission, mindset, and practice. Kind of like building a new habit or strengthening a muscle.

HELPFUL NUDGES

Jill was a successful executive at a large tech company after navigating her way through the ranks to a position that didn't satisfy her. Her company offered sabbaticals to employees at certain milestones, and Jill had been eligible for several years. She'd been reluctant to take a sabbatical, worried that she would miss out on future opportunities and be leapfrogged by others vying for similar roles. Plus, there was the frightening truth that she hadn't seen other women successfully take sabbaticals and return to elevated roles in the company.

Some of her friends encouraged her to take advantage of the opportunity. Thanks to their nudges, she eventually overcame her fear and took the sabbatical.

During the sabbatical, she took time to breathe. She explored her interests and stumbled into opportunities that eventually landed her in a completely unexpected place. She left her secure position at the tech company, much to her parents' chagrin, and has embarked on a venture of her own where, she said, "I am living my soul's purpose."

This is a far cry from where she was at the tech company.

She expresses gratitude on a regular basis for her friends' nudging (and her husband's) that pushed her to the point where she got out of her head and made the decision. It all started with making herself the priority and then giving herself permission to take a step back.

At times when we struggle, we can all use a friend, coworker, or family member nudging us to focus on our needs.

YOUR LIFE, YOUR RULES

After an early period of midlife angst, Amy figured out how to be happy. Turns out, it's a choice.

"After divorcing, I realized at forty that I didn't feel the need to have kids, in spite of societal expectations. I wouldn't mind marrying again someday, but because I don't feel the need to have children, I'm not in a hurry to remarry right away."

After using hypnosis to create a positive association with being alone, she's become comfortable with it. She's been intentional about who she surrounds herself with and likes the life she's created. While she feels unconventional at times, she owns her journey. When she threw herself a fortieth birthday party, her parents saw all her friends and stopped worrying about her. At this point, she's grown accustomed to *not* being like everyone else.

Her life, her rules.

You may be saying, *But it's different for me because I have kids,* or *It's different for me because I'm married,* or *single,* or *not rich.* The list can go on and on.

To this, I say, "Yes, and . . ."

We all have constraints that may limit our freedom, but it's not an all-or-nothing proposition. We can put ourselves first, be honest about what we want, and set our own rules.

It's time to rewrite the rules and create ones that work better for us.

We women live in a world that wasn't designed by us or for us. Very often, we don't have a voice in a lot of what happens in this world. This, too, is changing.

My friend Marie is fifty-one and is loving her fifties. She said, "I was finding my voice in my forties, but really found it when I turned fifty. I turned off the edit button. I discovered what I wanted to say, and I wanted to get out into the world. I love meeting women in their fifties because they, like me, are so over everything. We are done diminishing ourselves to make others feel better about themselves."

If that isn't inspirational, I don't know what is.

She didn't get there easily or magically when she blew out the candles on her fiftieth birthday cake. Her husband left her, and she's done serious personal development work.

I asked her, "Could you have made these discoveries with your ex-husband in your life?"

"If he had been supportive," she said, "then yes, but he wasn't. I think he struggled with me stepping into my own light and space. He'd gotten used to me stepping back and pushing him forward. Being in the background no longer worked for me."

She is responsible for financially and emotionally supporting herself and her teenage son. When a night workout class that she wanted to attend popped up, she felt reluctant to leave him. "It's only an hour once a week," she said, "but I was concerned about leaving him alone. He encouraged me to go. He is 100% supportive and paying attention to everything I am doing. He sees the changes. He sees me getting happier and stronger."

Many of the women I interviewed talked about how important it is to define what you want, make yourself the important project, and care about your own happiness, even though it will disrupt others.

We need to buck social norms and expectations around what it means to be a woman, a wife, a mom, to simply *be* in this world. It's time we rewrite the rules to suit our needs and not make everyone else less uncomfortable.

It's OK to choose you.

LIMITING BELIEFS

Fired up yet?

Ready to get started on choosing you?

As you think about what you want your life to be, don't be surprised if negative and nasty thoughts pop up in your brain.

In high school, my soccer coach said that I would never be successful in romantic relationships. At the time, I was determined to be the CEO of a Fortune 500 company and had decided that if I wasn't going to marry a guy or he wasn't a ton of fun, he wasn't worth my time or effort. I was a bit cutthroat in the way I approached relationships, which, admittedly, was a bit odd, but still, who says this to a sixteen-year-old girl?

Nearly ten years later, I made a list of what I wanted in a husband and ended up marrying my now-husband about a year later. This was after three failed dating attempts between the ages of thirteen and twenty-four. He knew long before I did that we were meant for each other. We've been married twenty-three years, have two teenage children, and are rapidly approaching being empty-nesters ready to embark on the next phase of our relationship.

While I didn't become CEO of a Fortune 500 company, I've been successful professionally on my own terms. Despite what my soccer coach thought and said, my husband and I have a solid relationship. I didn't let my coach's belief hold me back or limit me. Although it still puzzles me.

We don't just manufacture these limiting beliefs out of thin air. Limiting beliefs can come from others who appear to be helpful, supportive, and concerned. That could be limiting you. It's bad enough when we limit ourselves, but we absolutely cannot let someone else's limiting beliefs become our own!

When I talk to my mom about scary things, she may inadvertently create limits for me because of her fears. She doesn't want to see me hurt or fail; as a mother, I get this. She isn't intentionally holding me back, of course. But if I listen to her limiting beliefs, I'll end up cheating myself out of opportunities and experiences.

We "decide" to believe in limiting beliefs, sometimes consciously and sometimes not.[11] These beliefs become the things that run our lives. Author Louis L. Hay said, "We learn our belief systems as very little children, and then we move through life creating experiences to match our beliefs. Look back in your own life and notice how often you have gone through the same experience."

Our brains are powerful tools—and weapons. Limiting beliefs show up as doubts and falsehoods about our self-identity. Not only can we let go of some of our limiting beliefs, but we can create positive beliefs to give us the lift we need to create our ideal life.

One of the best examples I have is taken from my identical twin sister.

My sister and I separated the world a long time ago. She went the science route, and I went the business route. She liked chocolate, and I liked vanilla. I dated a lot in high school; she didn't. I played the cello; she played the violin. She ran cross-country and track; I was a cheerleader and played softball. When I was younger, people would say I was the pretty one, and my sister was the cute one. Some even said that she was the smart one, but that was wrong. We were both smart.

I never let that one limit me.

Unbeknownst to us, we put ourselves into boxes while trying to solve the problem of carving out our own identities. We created yet another box because we set boundaries around what we could do or how we saw ourselves in the world.

The walls of these boxes have broken down over the years because, despite our beginnings, we've exchanged paths. Or, more accurately, have blended them. For twenty years, I've worked with life science companies, and I spend a lot of time thinking about health and science. She opened a wine shop a number of years ago with a business partner. The lines have blurred in how we define ourselves and our worlds.

EXAMPLES OF LIMITING BELIEFS

So, really, what are examples of limiting beliefs, and how does one get past them?

Some of the most common examples include the following. Keep in mind that the language around them can be a lot more colorful, subtle, and deceptive.

- I'm not good with money.
- I'm not a risk-taker.
- I'm not disciplined.
- I don't have time.
- I'm too old.
- I don't have enough money.
- I've tried that before, and it didn't work.

- I'm not _____ enough. (Smart, funny, thin, etc.)
- I'm going to fail, so why bother trying?
- I don't do that kind of thing. That's not me.

In the article "4 Steps to Release 'Limiting Beliefs' Learned From Childhood,"[12] Matt James included a list of incredibly useful steps to understand and get past limiting beliefs:

1. Write the limiting belief down. This may take some digging to get to the belief, but it's worth the effort.
2. Acknowledge that these are *beliefs* and not *truths*.
3. Try on a different belief. Twist the belief around, or turn it on its head. One example he gives is: "My financial difficulties in the past have taught me so much that I'm fully prepared to handle them now!"
4. Take a different action by assuming the new and different belief is true.

This is an area where taking small steps may trigger a domino effect. Give it a try, and see what happens. You might surprise yourself. No, you *will* surprise yourself. And, if you let it, it will give you greater confidence to keep going.

IMPORTANCE OF CHOICE

My high school English teacher, Anne Parris, had my trust and adoration.

She taught me her first year of teaching and the following three years. I tortured her with sexual references in pretty much everything I wrote, the poor woman, but I was always engaged in her classes. She exposed me to fun and unorthodox literature, including *Rosencrantz and Guildenstern Are Dead*. While many of the books I read in her class left a huge impression on me, this one taught me the unforgettable lesson around choice.

Because of her, I learned that by not making a choice, you are, in fact, making a choice.

As a result, I am fairly decisive. My daughter, on the other hand, hates making decisions, which drives me batshit crazy. Thanks to her, I have realized that for some people, making decisions can be difficult. Specifically, choosing something in *our* best interest can be hard. It takes practice. Thankfully, it seems to get easier over time, and it's important to be intentional.

One of the gals I interviewed talked about how she reclaimed her life. She said, "Once I realized I had choice, the locus of control came back to me."

Just as Maxine Waters reclaims her time on the House floor, we need to reclaim our right to choose, and then own that decision.

Randi Levin, a Transitional Life Strategist based in NYC, uses a beautiful metaphor about being the CEO of our own lives in an episode of the Covey Club podcast. Just as the buck stops with the CEO, the buck stops with us when we own our decisions, our dreams, our actions, and our beliefs.

TRUST ABUNDANCE

The article "10 Steps to Develop and Model an Abundance Mindset" summarizes abundance perfectly. The abundance mindset is *a concept in which a person believes there are enough resources and successes to share with others.*[13] Life is not pie; the table can always be bigger, and there's plenty available. This is the opposite of the *mine, mine, mine* mentality where there's only so much available; if someone else gets it, you get none of it.

Life is not a zero-sum game.

This goes back to limiting beliefs. We can manifest more by trusting there is enough of what we need, when we need it. When we're afraid that there's not enough, we tighten up in body and mind. We limit what may be available to us. When we have an abundance mindset, *it opens possibilities, options, alternatives, and creativity.*[14]

The article also included a list of what becomes available with an abundance mindset:

- Live an unlimited, full, and satisfying life.
- Exude happiness despite circumstances.
- Give and receive affection and items of high value with ease.
- Feel plentiful, creative, and inspired.
- Take full advantage of and enjoy new opportunities that come your way.
- Create memorable and meaningful life experiences.
- Feel secure and confident in your life endeavors, and create successful outcomes.

When we go through transitional times and feel uncomfortable with where we are, it's easy to take on the scarcity mentality or think that there's never going to be enough. Fear has a way of bringing us to that mind space.

Sometimes we just have to breathe, talk ourselves off the ledge, and trust in abundance.

BE SELFISH

As part of creating lift, we need to lose the guilt. It weighs us down.

Most of us are raised to be generous, but women are more often taught to put others first. To not take the last piece of cake. To never be the first one in a buffet line.

When I became a mother, society told me that I needed to put my child first. Even working was being selfish—even though I had to work to provide for my child. I struggled to take time for myself because that would deprive my child of his mother.

When my husband left his job to stay home with the kids, I

continued to feel guilty about taking time for myself. In my mind, I rationalized it by thinking that I had accepted my choice to have kids; therefore, I had to accept the personal sacrifices that came with it. I worked a lot, and any time I spent on myself felt wrongly selfish and became laden with guilt.

Oh, how I wish I'd let go of that guilt a long time ago. Nowadays, I don't feel guilty about taking time for myself, largely because the kids are older and would probably rather I wasn't around as much.

Society fails women by teaching us this false narrative and expectation. There is a lot to be said for putting on your own oxygen mask first. You can't be there for anyone else if you don't take care of yourself first.

I remember reading books as a teenager that encouraged girls to put their boyfriends before themselves and celebrated unselfish women. I'd like to see those books burned. The boys of my generation (and of my dad's generation) were not fed the same bullshit. My husband has no problem getting up in the morning and making sure he gets his coffee, eats his breakfast, and reads the newspaper without thinking about anyone else in the household. He does so without any guilt.

I was raised to bring a hostess gift when I go to someone's house and to send a thank-you note after the event. This doesn't occur to my husband. It's a continuation of the expectation that girls should be thoughtful and considerate in ways that boys are not.

Recently, a friend and colleague of mine came to my house for coffee instead of the local coffee shop. She showed up with a smile and a daffodil plant.

"Why the plant?" I asked, pleasantly surprised.

"Because I can't show up to someone's house empty-handed."

Next time we're meeting at the coffee shop.

These types of activities are generally a female burden, which consumes energy and bandwidth that could be spent on something like . . . I don't know . . . *ourselves*? Let's campaign to reclaim this time! It should be spent without guilt and with a redefinition of selfishness.

Selma Blair spoke about getting her multiple sclerosis diagnosis in an interview, and mentioned how she was somewhat relieved to finally have an answer. That answer gave her permission to rest, deal with her illness, and not feel guilty. Prior to the diagnosis, she felt ashamed if she didn't do it all.

We can't win.

Which is why it's so important for us to claim our space and our time without guilt—and to be selfish. Let's redefine the term *selfish* into one of self-care, and not one of harming others.

A friend invited me for dinner the other night, so I brought cut flowers from our garden and a bottle of champagne to drink. I actually walked in and apologized for only bringing the flowers without a vase and nothing else but the champagne. After expressing her gratitude for the gifts, she told me about a friend who felt she must bring something significant, like a roast, every time she came over—even if dinner was already made. This totally screwed-up dynamic actually creates a greater burden for the hostess and an endless cycle of thank-you notes.

The bottom line here: we can put ourselves first while maintaining an awareness of our impact on others. By doing so, we eliminate guilt. When we stop trying to overcompensate, and let our presence shine, our brilliance will be enough.

And damn it, be the first in the buffet line, and take the last fucking cupcake.

CELEBRATE BEING FEMALE

I sometimes wonder if my daughter decided that being female is too hard and, therefore, is rejecting her gender. Or maybe she just doesn't want to be labeled based on her gender, which is very Gen Z. Right now, it's not that she wants to be a boy; she just doesn't want to be labeled a girl. She prefers nonbinary. I am still getting used to this concept for my child.

I know that, for many, this is not a choice; it is simply who they are. I absolutely support that. For Rei, I am not so sure. I see this as part of a broader search into how she sees herself and who she wants to be in this world. Some kids have always known. Some kids have questions and need to explore. I think she's still figuring it out and that it's fluid for her right now. Maybe it will always be.

I worry that some of this questioning stems from my sharing too much about how challenging it is to be female. My son thinks that I'm far too pro-women and that, somehow, he'll lose if women gain. We didn't raise him with a scarcity mentality, but we did have to say over and over again that Rei's existence and success don't detract from his existence or success.

The Science Vs podcast released an episode titled "The Science of Being Transgender." It discusses how science has been getting gender wrong for decades. They've mixed up gender with genitalia.

When I think about Rei and her gender-identity exploration, I wonder how much of what we have talked about, how we have raised her, and what she is exposed to affects how she sees herself in the world.

Did I inadvertently make one child resent me for celebrating women and the other afraid to be a woman? Or is it just who she is?

The Gen Z generation doesn't see gender defining them as much as previous generations. For those of us raised in societies where gender not only mattered but also limited our opportunities (whether we wanted to admit it or not), being a woman has mattered.

For years, I rejected the idea of being female, thinking that being male was better. My best friends in high school were guys, and I often felt more comfortable around them. I didn't want to be part of the girls' drama. I also wanted to compete with the boys. In elementary school, I practically bullied the boys to show that I was stronger, faster, better. Even then, I knew that it wasn't a level playing field, but I refused to accept that I couldn't do as well as my male counterparts. I still refuse to accept this.

At thirty-seven, I realized there were unseen obstacles for me that weren't in place for the men. In some cases, subtle microaggressions made me feel like I was crazy. I remember thinking that, no matter what I did, certain doors wouldn't be open to me. The glass ceiling really did exist. And if you were a working mom, it was even worse.

Until that time, I thought I controlled my destiny and no one could get in my way. This recognition was actually freeing, despite the external limitations.

A few years later, I read the book *Feminist Fight Club* and realized that I wasn't crazy. I'd been subjected to subtle sexism for years, and I wasn't alone. Somewhere in between, I realized that being a woman was pretty awesome and decided to embrace my femininity and see it as a strength and not as a weakness. I began to strip away all of the behaviors and thoughts (adaptations and accommodations) that I'd used to avoid being seen as a woman.

A life coach helped me get back in touch with my intuition (one of a woman's greatest assets), and I continue to strip away the things that aren't authentically me. I felt like I had been apologizing for being a woman instead of celebrating it. I still love hanging out with the guys, but I don't try to be one anymore.

There are some really cool things that are inherently female and need to be celebrated, including bearing children, breastfeeding, and female orgasms.

Yes, you read that right. Women may have better orgasms than men (something I read a long time ago that I can definitely relate to) and if not better, definitely longer. Women's last, on average, twenty seconds, while men's last three to ten seconds, according to an Australian health study in 2001-2002.[15] I can believe that. (Skip to chapter sixteen for more on sexploration!)

As I embrace being a woman and making choices based on what I want (and not just fitting in with the guys), I will order the foofy cocktail or a glass of champagne. I will push for events to be created for women with things I like, such as flowers, champagne, comfortable chairs designed for women wearing skirts, and places to put my purse, and not beer and football. Yes, that's a stereotype and a generalization, but I am sick of investor events being tailored to and advertised for men without any consideration to what women may want/need. I will choose what I want regardless of the optics.

Because I think it's fucking awesome to be a woman.

I'll Cry If I Want To

A founder I love wrote an article titled, "Why It Is Okay to Cry in the Workplace." She talked about being an empath and how she has to feel something before she can think about it. Sometimes she has to cry as part of her process.

Some of us get mad and cry. When we do so, it's frowned upon in professional, social, and even some private settings. How many times have you cried only to have the other person distance themselves like you have the plague? Maybe that's just me.

As we shift into a new place, we often experience new and potentially powerful feelings. Rev. Connie Habash often talks about the importance of *letting feelings flow through you like a wave.*

For so many of us, we want to resist and avoid our difficult feelings. But if we do, she says, "the fear builds up." We need to be intentional about sitting with the discomfort. We need to have faith in ourselves, knowing that we can handle it. When we let the fear, the yucky feelings, and the discomfort just be, eventually, like the wave, they will recede and dissipate.

If we keep holding them or avoiding them, they are going to come back, often more powerfully than before.

Other people may be afraid of my feelings, but I'm no longer afraid of them. It's taken a lot of years to get to this place, but it's so worth it.

The other day while mad and frustrated about something, I yelled about it. My husband recoiled, then leaned in and said, "Chill out."

I have zero tolerance for being talked over, mansplained, or told to calm down. "I'm not mad at you," I said, which helped him relax. I continued, "I'm mad and frustrated, and I want to yell."

He stood there expressionless until I was done and then said, "Well, that must be frustrating."

I enjoy having a full range of emotions, and I feel more complete because of them. I'm not going to hold them back or apologize for them because they make someone else uncomfortable. If you've been holding back, you have my full permission to feel the feels and emote in a way that works for you. Anyone offended or uncomfortable can get over their damn selves.

DECISION. PERMISSION. FEARLESSNESS.

Once you've decided you're deserving, discover you want it, and give yourself permission to take action, it's all about permission. Reminding yourself of your decision may be necessary.

Every damn time.

When Jill was twenty-six, she encountered her first failure: she divorced her high school sweetheart after two years of marriage. Her ex-husband called her selfish when she decided that her happiness was important.

While she couldn't see that she was unhappy, her friends could. They reminded her that she was once happy and deserved to be happy again. Not only had she forgotten how to be happy; she'd forgotten about her own powers, including giving herself permission. In this case, it was the permission to be happy.

She took it a few steps further and became fearless in her determination to define *her* life the way she wanted it.

Over time, as she climbed the corporate ladder and found professional success, she forgot about her permissive power again. She was so focused on trying to prove her worth to others that she'd lost sight of her own values and happiness. At the start of her midlife journey at forty-one, she remembered.

She took a much-needed sabbatical and rebalanced her life. She started doing work that aligned with her values. "I am choosing to be more conscious of my thoughts and how they affect my choices," she said. "I'm being more intentional with my time and who I spend it with. I want women to feel supported, which means I want to graciously give time to other women to support their dreams and ambitions. I want part of my legacy to be being seen as a woman who supported other women."

She is back to choosing what she wants in her life, giving herself permission to be happy, and fearlessly pursuing new dreams. She has big plans that can be daunting at times, but she knows she's on the right path.

"What do you do when you feel wobbly?" I asked.

"I reach out to my friends and other supportive people in my life," she said. "Including my husband. One friend in particular believes that no problem is too big and that every problem has a solution. She is always there to brainstorm with me. I also make time to sleep because I find that everything is better after sleep."

As for permission, she said, "You have to revisit permission every once in a while because it's easy to build up resistance against it. Giving yourself permission takes practice. It also requires trust and a big shot of fearlessness."

TAKING THE CONTROLS

— What are some of my limiting beliefs?
— What rules do I need to rewrite to better serve me?
— Do I need to give myself permission to choose what I want and live my life?

BRIEFING NOTES

CONTROL IS AN ILLUSION

A series of whimsical prints by Brian Andreas hang in my office so that I can refer to them when I get hung up on something. Mostly they are there to remind me to be less serious—not the easiest task.

One of them has a gal sitting in an umbrella, leaning back, with her hair blowing in the wind and feet up in the air while holding onto the handle. Rather than holding the umbrella upright, she's sitting in it as one would a sailboat, letting the wind carry her, just as the water would carry someone in a boat.

> *If you hold on to the handle, she said, it's easier to maintain the illusion of control. But it's more fun to just let the wind carry you.*

For me, letting go of control feels risky. But as the quote says, control is just an illusion. Letting go has just as much of a chance to lead to something good as it does to something bad.

It's all in how we frame it in our minds.

CHAPTER 6
ELIMINATING DRAG, PART 1

When I fly, I pay attention to weather, air traffic, safe landing spots in the event of an engine failure, and the condition of the helicopter. I regularly scan the cockpit to confirm I have enough fuel, that the oil and temperature gauges are within range, and that there are no warning lights indicating a problem. I also pay attention to how the helicopter is operating because things like drag affect overall performance, including fuel consumption and speed.

Drag is a real problem—literally and figuratively.

There are three types of drag that work against the helicopter: parasitic, profile, and induced. The first two are caused by resistance, and the latter is the result of the lift that gets the helicopter off the ground and keeps it there. Counteracting the first two is all about streamlining. For the third, it's all about movement.

Women face a significant amount of resistance in our daily lives that can affect our overall performance and quality of life. It can change the way we see ourselves, can be draining emotionally and physically, and may even limit what we do in the world.

Some of this drag is self-imposed. It's in the way we see ourselves. It's in the way we set expectations. It's the limits we set on ourselves (like thinking we don't have what it takes to accomplish our dreams). It's in the way we *think* we need to make choices.

It's time to appreciate our own value.

Time to throw off societal expectations and be who we are or want to be. Time to let go of the guilt that keeps us from making ourselves the priority. We can support each other and prevent drag from happening to others. We don't have anything to prove anymore.

You are enough. I am enough.

We are enough.

APPRECIATING OUR VALUE

Women rarely believe in their own value.

We talk ourselves out of doing something because we feel like we need another certification or degree, or it will take too much time, or we aren't worth the expense. We don't feel like we are enough. Social media doesn't help. If we let ourselves get caught in the comparison game, everything falls apart.

We box ourselves in with our own limiting beliefs.

Julie Gordon White, whom I mentioned in chapter two, helps her female clients destroy limiting beliefs and understand their value. How do I know? Because I was one of her clients. She taught me to look beyond what I think is possible. She says, "If you can think of it, it's for you. You have to trust it."

We sometimes struggle to ask for the compensation we want (and deserve), or to bill clients at rates that are aligned with our worth because, she says, "We're afraid no one will buy our services, pay the fees, or hire us."

But they will, and they do.

It's all about having the courage to take the first step.

She says, "Far too often, they [her clients] are thinking too much about themselves and not about their impact. This is where they get stuck. Once they have the confidence to take the first step, they get unstuck."

Once we're unstuck, we can get out of our heads, see our progress, and appreciate what we bring to the world.

We can appreciate our own value and ask for what we want and deserve.

BROADWAY, BABIES, AND BRAINS?

Jessica was living in New York City, dancing professionally, enjoying newly married life, and having the time of her life. She worked as part of a dance troupe and was set to perform around the world.

Then, at thirty-one, she found out she was pregnant.

She thought she had to decide between being a dancer headed for Broadway and having a baby. She chose the baby and moved to California so her husband could pursue his tech dreams. Although she never saw herself as a suburban mom dressed in sweatpants, she found herself living that life and feeling a little bit lost. She had her second child and still felt unfulfilled and trapped. Both she and her marriage suffered.

Then she discovered pole dancing and regained her sense of self. By dancing again, she was able to express herself in ways she hadn't since she left NYC. She felt revitalized. Her marriage flourished again. She regained her sense of self and the woman she thought she'd left behind in NYC.

Then she remembered that she also liked to use her brain.

Broadway, babies, brains . . . she didn't see a way for all of these to fit into her life at the same time. Eventually, the pendulum swung way over to the brain side that she previously thought couldn't coexist with her sexy dancing or mom sides.

She saw all of these as *or*, not *and*.

After forty, she realized these could exist at the same time. She didn't have to choose between being a good mother, a good dancer, or a smart businesswoman. She could be all of them. She is still learning how to balance, because the *and* concept is still relatively new.

For most of us, it's a spectrum. I prefer to see it as three-dimensional, with more points closer together—kind of like a prism or a

84

diamond. All facets can exist in the same object. It's just a matter of turning a degree or two to reflect a new facet.

It also allows us to shine bright and beautiful.

Jessica also learned that some doors can be reopened. Last year, the opportunity to live her dream of performing on Broadway became a reality. Yes, *that* Broadway. Not off-Broadway.

She went back to NYC to visit the choreographer of the show she left when she was thirty-one. The choreographer asked her to sit in on some auditions for the part Jessica had danced—which had been created just for her.

At the end of the auditions, the choreographer wasn't happy. She asked Jessica if she would do a performance in July, three months later, on Broadway.

"My initial response was *no,* even though I'd wanted this my whole life," Jessica explained to me. "I called my mom, who said I shouldn't do it. She said I'd already had my chance and that it was going to be too hard on my family. That the kids needed me. I decided to do it anyway. My mother's fear has never been my fear. I called my husband, somewhat afraid of his response, and he said, 'I guess we are going to New York City.'"

She went on to say, "It was a five-week gig, so I brought my daughter the first week so she could see where she was born and where we lived before we moved to California. I wanted her to see the park we went to when she was a baby. I made it all about her."

Then she lived her dream. She performed in a bikini on Broadway at the age of forty-two. Her husband and son were in the audience. She loved it. "I felt like I was reclaiming a part of me I thought was lost forever."

She also said, "I am working on finding my healthy spot. This means being able to slide on the continuum between sexy and smart. It's no longer a matter of one or the other."

Never one to settle in one place, Jessica completed a master's degree and is actively pursuing ways to bring her experience, education, and passion together to create something that other women can benefit from too.

BALANCING ACT

Jeanne was in her early thirties when she left her corporate gig to pursue yoga and ended up learning to teach. She ultimately launched a yoga studio business in Singapore and left her life in the U.S. to build that business.

"I found personal clarity after I left corporate. I wanted to pursue my dream of making people's lives better through yoga. Singapore was the next market for hot yoga and was very compelling from a business perspective."

Jeanne was living in Singapore, running multiple businesses, when her brother had a stroke.

"I became his legal guardian and oversaw his eighteen-month recovery. I dropped everything in Singapore to move to Chicago to become my brother's health advocate," she said. I asked her if she had a tendency to go all-in when she was faced with a challenge or opportunity. She reflected on that for a moment and then said, "Yes, I guess I do. I try to be more deliberate now and be more grounded."

While she was taking care of her brother, she thought she could oversee her business from the U.S. "I thought I could trust the woman I left in charge but was surprised to learn she'd been lying to me and stealing from me." Eventually, Jeanne went back to Singapore and shut down her businesses. She returned to the U.S. feeling like she'd failed.

Her brother recovered enough to move into a skilled nursing facility and no longer needed her 24/7. She was free to take care of herself. She moved back to San Francisco to pick up the pieces of her life and started her business, *Mighty Menopause*, to provide education and resources for women going through the menopause transition. (Yes, you've heard of her before, back in chapter four.)

She said, "At fifty-one, I don't have it all figured out, but I am looking for more balance. I am creating a happier and more joyful life for myself and helping women in the process. I don't have to choose between my business and my sanity. I can have both."

STOP CREATING DRAG FOR EACH OTHER

Differences between Baby Boomer and Gen X women in business are stark.

Baby Boomer women fought their way to *the* seat at the table. There was only one spot for one woman, and they clawed, scratched, and fought to not only get it, but to keep it. This often meant they had to make it difficult for other women to succeed, or they would lose that one seat.

I am very thankful to these women. If they hadn't done this work, our generation of women and the women behind us wouldn't have the opportunities that we do. We would still be fighting for that one spot.

Unfortunately, it's been difficult for some to shift from the scarcity mentality of a single seat at the table to one of abundance. They sometimes struggle to see that we can create a new or bigger table with plenty of seats. Or just create a completely different seating arrangement.

Comfy, cushioned chairs around a fire table with good lighting, anyone?

I wonder if this explains why it didn't occur to them to share what we women should expect in our forties and fifties. Perhaps they thought that since they had to figure it out on their own, we should have to do the same. Or maybe there were social constraints that made it more difficult for them to talk about these things. Or both.

We have the opportunity to change this situation by not only sharing with each other what we're experiencing so we feel less isolated and alone, but just as importantly, so we leave a legacy of information for the women coming behind us. We can provide the power of information and support to counteract the natural drag of life.

TAKING THE CONTROLS

— Do I appreciate my value and my worth?
— Do I make room for other women at the table?

BRIEFING NOTES

....
....
....
....
....
....
....
....
....
....
....
....
....
....
....
....
....
....
....
....
....
....

I AM A GIVING ADDICT

Every morning, I read an entry in a book on mindfulness. One day, an entry titled the *Life of a Caregiver* popped up that was perfect for that particular day. I'd posed some questions in my morning pages the previous day around the topic.

Here's what I learned: giving isn't always generosity.

Mind blown!

As girls, we are socialized to be the caretakers, to help others, and we are celebrated for it until there's nothing left of us. We are taught and conditioned to believe that being selfish is a major no-no and that *to not give is to be selfish.*

When I was in high school, my parents called me the ice princess. For years, they got on my case about not being compassionate and caring enough. Looking back, I think I was compassionate and caring, but I also cared about *me.* I spent years trying to compensate for this perceived character flaw by giving to others to show how generous, compassionate, and caring I was until it became, as I learned, an addiction.

Now, before I agree to give something to someone else, I try to ask myself a few questions:

- Why am I giving this?
- Am I doing this to compensate for something else?
- Am I doing this to look good?
- Am I doing this because it's easier to say *yes* than *no*?
- How do I really feel about this?

It's not easy. I catch myself agreeing to things that I really wish I hadn't. The other day, I received a text from someone asking us for something, and I said *yes* without thinking. Then my husband asked, "Why did you even respond to that? You know you don't want to do it, nor do you need to."

Ugh. He was totally right. Fortunately, he helped me get out of it gracefully.

I must think there's some sort of universal tally system and that I am always at a deficit. I don't know why I think that I need to make up for an overdrawn account. It's not like I let others give much to me, creating a natural give-and-take. Receiving feels uncomfortable, but I'm working on that too.

I wonder if I will ever let it be in balance.

CHAPTER 7

ELIMINATING DRAG, PART 2:

LETTING GO OF WHAT NO LONGER SERVES YOU

In the previous chapter, I talked about the internal or external resistance that drags us down on a daily basis. In this chapter, it's all about letting go of the friction we create by not letting go of things, behaviors, thoughts, and people that no longer serve us.

As I explored the topic of letting go, I found an article titled "8 Exercises to Help You Let Go of the Things That No Longer Serve You"[16] that categorized our life (stuff) into four areas:

1. **Internal:** beliefs, values, goals, duties, obligations
2. **Behavioral:** habits, hobbies, pursuits, commitments
3. **Physical:** possessions, ownership
4. **People:** relationships, roles, groups, connections

Throughout our lives, we create attachments and become burdened by them. We hang on because we're afraid. We grow comfortable with the familiar, regardless of whether it's good for us.

Then we suffer.

It's helpful—no, vital—that we periodically analyze and assess the areas in our lives and make sure the *stuff* there still fits. To make room for better, we have to let go of the old. It isn't just a matter of letting go of what no longer serves us, but also letting go of what may be harmful to us.

We live in a society where accumulation seems to be the name of the game. Yet, "the less you hold, the more your hands are open to what's here, unexpected, and transformative. In every moment is the possibility for a new discovery, a radical undoing," says Jan Frazier, author of "The Freedom of Being: At Ease with What Is."

"8 Exercises to Help You Let Go of the Things That No Longer Serve You" also says, "It's okay to let things go. It's okay to admit that something used to work, and now it doesn't. It's okay to change. It's okay to require change."

In other words, it's OK to change our minds. But where does one start? This can feel so overwhelming.

We have to Marie Kondo our *lives* and not just our homes.

RECOGNIZING WHERE PERFECTION COMES FROM

The drive toward perfection seems to be the bane of nearly every woman's existence.

As young girls, we're rewarded for complying with the rules, not being disruptive, getting good grades, not being difficult, and constantly striving for perfection. Conflicting information on the source of this phenomenon is plentiful. One author says we did it to ourselves and that it's our own damn fault.

I completely disagree with this.

The issue is likely more basic than this and results from being told, for decades, that we don't belong. We internalize this subtle and overt messaging and hold ourselves to a high standard, "knowing that our missteps will be noticed more and remembered longer than those of our male peers."[17]

We endure an insufferable number of microaggressions that erode our confidence until *we* can't fully appreciate our own worth.[18] Then we seek external validation. We pursue more and more, better and better, without ever hitting the mark. Add imposter syndrome, and we suffer a spiral of psychological death and unhappiness.

Society holds us to unreasonable standards of youth and beauty. We aren't appreciated for our differences, which create a beautiful mix. We can appreciate the diversity of wildflowers, all contributing different colors, shapes, sizes, and fragrances.

Why not for women?

If our faces aren't perfect, we use makeup. We change our hair color, style, and length to hide or enhance ourselves. Heels elongate our legs, and push-up bras perk up our boobs. We're constantly encouraged to reach and strive for more. It's exhausting and unrealistic. All to make ourselves conform to society's perfect image of a woman.

Dr. Natalie Crawford discussed this problem with perfection that leads to confidence issues for girls in her podcast, *As A Woman*. She said, "Girls are more disciplined and goal-oriented at an earlier age than boys and want to get the answers right. Girls are rewarded for this behavior and also feel as if they're not good enough unless their answers are perfect. This means their confidence comes from *getting it right*. Boys, on the other hand, are rewarded for *trying*, and their confidence comes from the trying and not from the outcome."

And there it is, ladies. Our confidence and self-esteem are destroyed because:

- We were rewarded for getting it right at an early age.
- Society has unreasonably irrational expectations when it comes to our appearance and acceptable behavior.
- We suffer microaggressions about not belonging.

It's no wonder we are constantly playing the comparison game and coming up short!

So many of us bought into this damned myth and still battle it every day. My only hope is that the cycle begins to end with our generation.

STRIVE FOR EXCELLENCE, NOT PERFECTION

I feel better knowing that we battle generations of resistance and that it's not just me struggling to let go of the need to be perfect.

Every time I go flying, I want to cancel for fear of not being perfect. Crashing and dying don't even cross my mind, but I do worry about other people discovering that I don't know everything. To help with these self-doubts, I mitigate risk by bringing a seasoned pilot with me.

I passed all the tests and met all the requirements over ten years ago. Legally, no one else needs to fly with me.

I confessed to one of my favorite flight instructors during one of my last flights that the idea of screwing up terrifies me. He said, "That's normal. A lot of pilots feel this way."

I had no idea.

This reassured me, and I realized I should have said something sooner. Instead, I held myself to an impossible and unrealistic standard and stressed about it.

Meg Myers Morgan, Ph.D., says in her book *Everything is Negotiable*, "Perfectionism can make you perform well but also might make you feel like shit . . . Instead of seeking perfection, find your level best. Have standards, not impossible ones . . . Excellence is different from perfection. One can be achieved and maintained. The other cannot. Strive for excellence."

KILLING WONDER WOMAN

Tawana killed her inner Wonder Woman.

I wasn't sure how to react when she told me. I like the image of strength, beauty, magic, and sisterhood Wonder Woman represents. At the same time, Wonder Woman represents unrealistic expectations for women—especially Gen X women who were told we could have and be it all.

That's as big a myth as Wonder Woman herself.

Tawana spent so much time traveling (approximately three weeks out of the month), that she didn't know where she was at any given time. She didn't unpack when she returned home, and she never relaxed. Thanks to drinking wine every night, she gained weight and wondered if she was depressed. (Perimenopause + wine + heavy travel schedule!) She read Brené Brown's book on shame. That's when she realized something needed to change.

She uncharacteristically went to a moms' retreat with a hundred other women. The conversation about how they lived their lives arose. The coach said to her, "What you're doing and how you're living isn't good for you."

Tawana decided there had to be a better way and wanted to figure it out.

Tawana said, "I felt like things were happening *to* me, and I wasn't owning my life, my experience, or my feelings. I was on autopilot. I decided to reengage and penciled in time to reflect on what I wanted. I tried this for about six weeks, then extended it to twelve weeks."

She created a vision board, hired a life coach, and created goals. She thought her life coach would only help her professionally. I laughed aloud (not at her, mind you). Bev and I have talked at length about how the work we do in one part of our life bleeds over into the other areas of our lives.

As we continued to talk, Tawana said, "I was making changes in my life, and it was hard work. I continued to have questions, especially in my personal life, unrelated to my job. I stubbornly tried to keep my professional work compartmentalized and separate from my personal life."

After six weeks, she realized she had to let go and open the emotional work to all aspects of her life. She didn't have to have it all figured out. "This was so freeing to acknowledge. It was scary, too. I couldn't see where the path was going and had to trust I was doing the right thing. This was a time of awakening for me," she said, "and I appreciated the gift of choice and opportunity."

Her coach is helping her reframe how she talks to herself and sets expectations. She's created a new way of being after realizing how her previous behavior was harmful.

That is why she fired Wonder Woman.

The model didn't work for her anymore—though one could argue that the model doesn't work for any woman.

In rejecting Wonder Woman, she acknowledges being human. She is more honest about her abilities, weaknesses, and relationships. When she traveled less and did less, she had her best year at work. A promotion came. She was invited onto a board. She no longer goes into work on Fridays. Overall, she feels more complete and fulfilled.

Best of all, she is letting go.

PROJECT "I DON'T GIVE A FUCK"

I went to bed irate one night and woke up angry the following morning.

A *Simple Habit* meditation on anger helped me breathe through the rage I felt in bed. Through this, I realized the anger was a symptom of something bigger. For all of you enlightened women out there, stop laughing. This was new to me.

The meditation had me visualize the anger. I saw people I knew, starting with my family members. I'd been struggling with feeling a lack of support from my husband and my mother. A lack of recognition and acknowledgment for the work I'd been doing also made me resentful. I was sliding into feeling like a martyr, which I hate.

I moved from my bed to my yoga mat for my daily stretching and breathing and found another meditation on letting go of the past. As I used my Apple Watch to do one-minute breathing exercises, I started with child's pose and worked on letting go of expectations. Of disappointments. Of images of how things should be. Then I moved to the couch. After journaling about the anger, resentment, and lack of support, I set limits on myself. That's when I decided to start *Project "I Don't Give a Fuck."*

Seems a bit harsh, I know, but dark times call for harsh measures.

I want to internalize the feeling of not needing external validation to feel good. By doing so, I intend to remove my need to have other people validate my work, my existence, and my value.

I only have so many fucks to give, so I need to be judicious in how I use them.

It's all about energy management.

My hope is that with this project I can begin to recognize when I start to slip into the old patterns. I already feel better about having a plan in place, which is exactly what the meditation suggested . . . that by taking steps toward resolution, I can begin to see the anger dissipate.

So, when I start to slip, I can look into my jar of fucks and see if there are enough for it. And if not, I can let it go.

REFRAMING: SEEING THE BEAUTY IN AGING

Carmen was fifty when she started to quiet the voices in her head that had her constantly searching for meaning and purpose.

She had a successful career in management consulting and left her lucrative position to begin a startup. (Because that's what you do in Silicon Valley!) The startup was a total and complete failure, for which she is extremely grateful. The experience made her face her own limitations and define what she wanted.

At the same time, she started to see a decline in her looks, which she had always depended on. In the past, she would have hidden from the difficult emotions that came up, but this time, she decided not to. She chose to look inside of herself, take stock, and understand her values.

She and her husband had chosen not to have children and had the financial freedom for her to take time to figure her shit out. She started with breathing, meditation, and writing.

Her husband, mother, and friends thought she was losing it, but she didn't pay any attention to them. For the better part of a year, she continued to shed the things that no longer served her. She started to *feel* for the first time. She did research and eventually found shamanism. This led her to a retreat in Jamaica. She said, "The experience was transformational for both me and my husband."

She'd enjoyed painting when she was younger but had become very analytical and left-brained. She rediscovered her passion for art and picked up photography.

As she grieved for her lost self and looks, she used photographic self-portraits to discover herself in a whole new way. She said, "I learned to see the beauty in aging. I started to love who I had become."

She let go and accepted.

THERE ARE NO WINNERS IN THE COMPARISON GAME

Dr. Meg Myers Morgan, in her book *Everything is Negotiable,* says, "When it comes to getting what you want out of life, you'll find the biggest thing standing in your way is you. So, step aside." She found that women play the comparison game and are always coming up short. "Comparisons trick you into confusing your wants with someone else's," she said—which is so on point.

We'll never win the comparison game. Social media plays a major role in providing a fabulous platform (game board, anyone?) for the comparison game. To stop playing, Dr. Morgan suggests, "Own your abilities and your narratives around those abilities. Own everything you can, even your weaknesses."

Enough said.

FAILURE SHOULD BE YOUR SECOND FAVORITE F-WORD

Don't be afraid of failure.

Failure is part of human nature. If we're able to redefine failure as an opportunity to learn, we can use *failures* to create new opportunities.

Winston Churchill said it best when he said, "Success is not final; failure is not fatal: it is the courage to continue that counts."

Experiment.

Screw up.

Learn from it.

Apply the learning.

Move on.

No self-flagellation allowed.

You will fuck up. Accept it. Pick yourself up. Move on.

With some exceptions, I promise you will survive and be all the better for it.

RULES? WE DON'T NEED NO STINKING RULES

I think it's time to step back and ask yourself if the rules you are following:

1. Were set when you were five.
2. Are all in your head.
3. Really serve your life's purpose.

It's finally *your* time. You get to create the rules you want to live by, or change the rules if they no longer suit you.

- Eat cake for breakfast.
- Call in sick to work, and go to the beach.
- Delegate, hire, or abdicate dinner away.
- Wear white shoes after Labor Day. Pave a new fashion path!
- Don't go to church on Sundays. Give people something else to talk about.
- Tired of dyeing your hair, and want to go gray? Hey, silver foxy mama! Bring it!

Start paying attention to the so-called rules that constrain you. Question them. Then strip away what no longer serves you. Create new rules that work for you. Be open to continuing to change up the rules. They should evolve and grow as we do.

Don't go full anarchist. Just remember that it's *your* life.

TAKING THE CONTROLS

— Do I let perfection get in the way of my happiness?
— What can I learn from my latest failure?
— What *stuff* can I let go of?

BRIEFING NOTES

More Than My Name on a Mug

When I first started working for my dad's accounting firm as a teenager, I had a mug with my name and its meaning on it. I kept it for decades—it moved with me throughout my life, sometimes in a box, sometimes as my office mug, and other times in the kitchen cabinet.

Recently, I decided I didn't need a cup with my name on it to tell me who I was. I wrapped it up, put it in the Goodwill bag with a few other mugs, and gave it away. Now, I can clearly see my other mug options each day.

The universe decided to reward me for this. My husband picked up a new, bright red San Diego State University Mom mug when my son made his college decision. There's still room for one or two more that will spark joy each time I sip coffee or tea.

This reminds me of the story of the monkey that puts its hand into the hole of a coconut to grab a handful of rice. It ends up trapped. To get free, the monkey has to let go of the rice, but won't do it and remains trapped.

We can be like the monkey.

Sometimes, we hold on to things we think we need or want. When, really, they're dangerous or unhealthy. We hang on to assumptions, feelings, social constructs, expectations, people, and things.

Midlife is the perfect time to question all of these and ask, "What have you done for me lately?" If the answer is, "Nothing good," then it's time to let go.

MIRROR, MIRROR ON THE WALL . . .

I definitely struggle with the adjustment associated with my changing looks, and I know I am not alone.

Way too many advertisements for weight loss programs, exercise classes, Botox, sculpting, and more offer a magic fix to something there is no magic pill for. These companies see us resisting the aging process and capitalize on our fears and insecurities.

Stephanie Faubion, MD says, "Weight gain during midlife is common, and about two-thirds of women ages forty to fifty-nine and nearly three-quarters of women older than sixty are overweight."

This isn't only the result of hormone changes but is also due to the general aging process and reduced physical activity. We experience a change in estrogen that also leads to a shift of fat to the midsection.[19]

Add interrupted sleep and mood issues, and we have a hard time adhering to a healthy diet and exercise lifestyle. There are times that I say, "Screw it," and have a glass of wine (or three), and then decide to crawl into bed to read rather than getting on the treadmill.

My gynecologist sent me a video of an interview where a menopause expert talked about the hormonal and metabolic changes that make it so difficult to lose weight. I don't know if she sent it to me to make me feel better . . . or to better educate me. I learned there is no magic solution.

Great.

Once menopause hits, there is an opportunity to change. Is this permission to be where I am now, knowing that no matter what I do, I fight an uphill battle? Or do I say, "Challenge accepted," and fight like hell?

I haven't decided yet.

Researching more about what might work for your body is the best path. For me, this includes supplements, diet changes, a nutritional therapist, and possibly intermittent fasting or cutting down on my alcohol consumption.

The horror!

All of us have vastly different goals. My goal is to play tennis for three to four hours several days in a row without significant strain or recovery time. I want to be strong and flexible. I want to be able to go rafting or hiking up waterfalls without worrying if I am in good enough shape. Focusing on feeling good and strong rather than on what the scale says is helpful. I'm trying to look at myself in the mirror with gratitude for all life has provided, not focus on the lines, uneven skin tone, and age spots.

Damn, it's hard!

I may not walk into a room and command attention because of my looks the way I used to, but I can with my experience, accomplishments, sparkling wit, and personality. With time comes change, and I accept that.

These reflect well in the mirror and in life.

CHAPTER 8

ELIMINATING DRAG, PART 3: GRIEVING AND HEALING

We all carry a certain amount of baggage from our youth into midlife.

Thanks to midlife puberty, some of this baggage screams to be dealt with. It could be the changing hormones, the brain changes, or just a refusal to take this shit into the next phase of our life. Midlife spurs us to lighten our emotional load.

My friend Beth sent me some socks for my birthday that say, *Take no shit; give no fucks.* They motivate me to be clearer about what I want and care less about outside expectations.

It's not easy.

To let go of old baggage, we have to shine light on uncomfortable, painful, shameful, and/or disappointing aspects of our lives, then face them with honesty, grace, and compassion. Sometimes we need to grieve before we can heal, let go, or reframe. We may even grieve for what never was or what never will be. Then we can move on.

According to Mercy Cremations (morbid, I know), grief is a complex set of emotional, physical, spiritual, and intellectual reactions to loss. Amid this complexity, there's fear. We grieve because we have been painfully deprived of someone or something.

"We leave our old life; and for a time we wander; forging a path in the gap between the life now gone, and the new one we have yet to create . . . Grief is a natural part of our lives, and affects all aspects of our existence. It can cause us physical pain; and yet bring us to a deeper understanding of the true value and meaning of life. Grief can be very hard work; taking significant amounts of energy, it is a major force for change in our lives. We grieve naturally, which to us means it is a natural way for us to grow stronger and more resilient. But that certainly doesn't mean it's a pleasant path to take."[20]

Of course, there are the five stages of grief: denial, anger, bargaining, depression, and acceptance. But David Kessler writes about acceptance as the last stage in *accepting the new reality*.

"We learn to live with it," he says. "It is the new norm with which we must learn to live."

It's healthy—and expected—to let go of outdated expectations of ourselves, our lives, and other people. Then we can define what works best for us. It's hard, but necessary, work. Only through grieving for what can no longer be, can we create what we want for ourselves.

POSTPARTUM BRINGS EVERYTHING INTO FOCUS

Lindsay was taught that if you work hard enough, you can reach your goals. There was no room for excuses.

She discovered water polo in high school and became very good at it. She said, "My life revolved around water polo, and I was rewarded for my hard work and single-focused dedication with a scholarship to Stanford."

After graduation, she continued to focus on athletic pursuits, including triathlons and Iron Man competitions. She defined herself based on her athleticism . . . until her body told her it had reached its limit. She said, "I was pregnant with my second child, and my body fell apart. As I realized that I was never going to be able to compete at the same level as before, I started questioning who I was in the world."

Now, she struggles with twenty minutes on the elliptical, which is a far cry from where she was even on her lightest training days.

"I suffered from severe postpartum depression, which brought everything into focus. I kept wondering why parenting was so hard. Why it, too, couldn't just be trained through and figured out. Why was it so hard for me, but not for other moms?"

All the things that made her successful up until this point proved useless and often counterproductive to her recovery. She said, "This was the first time I couldn't see a way out of the situation. I assumed it would always be this way." She could no longer be who she used to be and didn't know who she was anymore.

The open field of possibilities terrified and overwhelmed her. She started asking herself the most basic questions about what she liked and wanted. She said, "I struggled to come up with the answers. I felt completely lost and had no idea where to begin."

She started working with a therapist to help her through the process, to let go of what could never be again, and continue to rebuild herself.

She has since had a third child and stumbled into community building at her kids' school, which she finds incredibly satisfying. While she can't go on the cycling rides she used to, and she misses them, she said, "I've learned to appreciate what my body does for me every single day, and I respect its limits."

"I grieved for the loss of who I was to make room for who I can and want to become."

COMPASSION FOR OUR YOUNGER SELVES

I've struggled with insecurity throughout my adult life, although I don't recall exactly when the struggle started. I wish I could say that I've figured out how to make this magically disappear, but I haven't. It's still a daily battle.

I think it all started during my freshman year of high school when I dated an emotionally destructive senior, who was toxic largely because of his own insecurities. My parents hated him and didn't want me to have anything to do with him. I wanted him all the more. That relationship probably would have ended eighteen months sooner if they had just let me date him.

I'd sneak out of the house to spend time with him at night

while my family slept. I thought he worshiped and adored me. I got caught up in what I thought was love and really great sex (I lost my virginity on my mother's birthday that summer). But his insecurities manifested in manipulative language used to undermine my self-esteem.

"You didn't bleed, so you must not have been a virgin."

"No one is going to want you now that you're no longer a virgin."

He looked at my stomach, which was not flat and had never been and said, "You need to lose weight."

Mind you, I was 5'5" and 105 pounds. My friend Stephanie and I restricted calories and lived on salads from the school salad bar, eating little else all day. Neither of us needed to lose any weight.

After he graduated, we continued to "not date" until sometime in my sophomore year. That's when I realized that the relationship wasn't healthy, and I ended up breaking it off. I distinctly remember Valentine's Day that year. He'd sent me some balloons and a teddy bear. Somewhere around that time, he called me and said, "Don't miss me when I'm gone."

"Where are you going?" I asked.

"Just don't miss me when I'm gone."

At that point, I immediately asked what he'd done and ended up sending an ambulance to his house. I don't recall whether he actually tried to hurt himself or not. At that point, I was done. The damage to my self-esteem was done too.

Some days, I feel as if I still grieve for the loss of my innocence. I was so young and impressionable and such a romantic. Sometimes I ask myself, "How could you have been so stupid?" and then I breathe and remind myself that I was fourteen and he was seventeen. Also, I had read way too many romance novels (starting with *Gone with the Wind*).

I look back at that girl and smile with sad compassion. She didn't know any better. She liked the external validation, perceived status, and prestige of an upperclassman being interested. It's time for me to stop judging my younger self and let her rest in peace, in my past.

MAKING ROOM FOR NEW FIRSTS

As we age, it can feel as if we've run out of positive and fresh firsts. Like the first kiss, first date, first day of college, first job, or first new car. First mammograms and colonoscopies don't count as positive firsts, by the way.

If you think about it, by trying lots of new things, we can create all the new *firsts* we want.

Recently, I participated in my very first protest (actually, it was an anti-protest since we were protesting the protesters at Planned Parenthood), and it felt great to do something new for the first time. Just like writing this book or starting my podcast.

In order to enjoy the new things in our lives without negative bias, we have to stop carrying negativity from the past. We need to honestly acknowledge our past experiences with compassion and gratitude. Compassion for our younger and more innocent selves. Compassion for the decisions we made. Gratitude for the experiences that have shaped our lives.

There is significant power in grieving and healing.

TAKING THE CONTROLS

— Am I suffering from old wounds from my childhood? From my twenties?

— What can I do to find peace and closure?

BRIEFING NOTES

....

....

....

....

....

....

....

....

....

....

....

....

....

....

....

....

....

....

....

....

....

....

WHO AM I?

As identical twins, my sister and I are considered the products of a genetic defect when, at the point of conception, the fertilized egg was too weak and split in two.

We fought for our own identities from day one. With names like Terri and Sherry, it was hard to be seen as individuals. We were the Twins, the Girls, the Hansons, Terri and Sherry the hairy blueberries (special thanks to Billy McNeil in fourth grade for this one).

We fought like crazy growing up but became best friends when we went off to separate colleges. This truce lasted until we were truly adults, and the fighting resumed in a much less obvious way. I stopped competing with her long ago and chose to live my own life, but our relationship continued to be challenged.

A few years ago, we fractured completely.

It's been a struggle to create my own identity as a *singlet* after over forty years of being a twin. I had to learn to live without her. For a long time, I felt as if part of my soul were missing—like I was incomplete. Adjusting to the change has been hard, and even harder knowing that I want the relationship when she doesn't.

We didn't even know we were identical until we were thirty-five and gave each other a DNA test for our birthday. I called her with the results, and she said, "Fuck you," and hung up on me. I called her back and left a voicemail letting her know that if she needed a kidney or blood, that I was her gal.

It took a while, but she eventually called me back and said, "I guess you're happy. You were right."

"I don't really care. It's just information."

She said, "Fuck you," and hung up on me again. I didn't see how this changed who we were or how the world perceived us.

But, to her, it mattered.

It's beginning to hurt less, but I still grieve for the close friendship that could have been. That really *should* have been. But I can't fix something that is outside of my control.

As we move through our lives, not everyone will stick with us. It's not always easy to let go of people, especially when no reason was given for them leaving us. But we can focus on our own lives, our own healing, and create relationships with others.

Even after the loss of a cell-sister.

CHAPTER 9

SETTING YOUR DESTINATION: THE SKY'S THE LIMIT

When we dream, we create excitement and improve our quality of life. Author Anna Marsh says, "You move beyond your current reality and develop new habits, as well as behaviors."

With a dream or a goal, "[people] stop focusing on what they don't have and pour their energy into what they want," says Mary Fukuda, CEO of N2 Publishing. "Mediocre goals never bring out greatness. Believe in yourself, and you can make anything happen."

I believe, I believe, I believe. (Maybe I should cut back on the wine while writing.)

If our lives are half over, what do we really have to lose (other than comfort, security, and our reputations)? What if we start "leaping off the cliff of the known and venturing into the wild depths of our truest longings," as yoga and meditation teacher Chad Woodford suggests?

What if . . . ?

If not now, when?

And what do we really want?

TENNIS WITH RICHARD BRANSON? WHY, YES, THANK YOU

Richard Branson is an avid tennis player.

When he's on Necker Island, he plays once or twice a day with one of his tennis pros. I, too, love to play tennis and decided shortly after I arrived at his personal paradise in 2016 that I would play tennis with him.

I spent nearly every day on the courts, foregoing other activities, hoping for my opportunity to open up. I shared my desire with Richard's tennis pro, Josh, who said he would help make it happen.

On our last full day on the island, we had a mini-Necker Cup tennis tournament. We rotated partners for each match and were nearing the end of the tournament. I still hadn't played with Richard despite being on the same team, the Flamingos. The other team was the Lemurs. (Both animals live on the island.) I was kicking myself for not having been braver and asking to play with him when I sat across from him at dinner the first night (after tripping and nearly falling into his lap).

Or asking him at breakfast the next morning.

Or at lunch the following day.

There had been plenty of opportunities to ask, but I didn't want to seem pushy. I assumed everyone wanted a piece of him, and I didn't want to be *one of those.*

Then the last match was announced, and I was paired with Richard. If we won, our team would celebrate by posing in front of the actual Necker Cup. If we lost, well, it was still a win for me.

There was a lot of laughter, especially after Richard got nailed by a ball at the net by the opposing team. (On that play, I was set to receive. The server hit the ball straight across the net and nailed Richard in the chest. Richard's immediate response was to flip off the server, which was surprising and left us all laughing.)

I played great, but we lost by one point. I still think we should have won automatically after Richard got hit at the net. As I said, it was still a win for me. I got to play tennis with a man I greatly admired on his private island after sharing my wish with Josh.

Magical things can happen when we put our wishes and desires into the universe, take steps to make them happen, and then grab the chances when they are offered to us.

GETTING OVER THE FEAR OF DREAMING

For my forty-eighth birthday, I came up with a vision for the impact I want to have in the world: *I want to live in a world where everyone has the opportunity to live freely, equally, and have an extraordinary life.*

Pretty simple, really. Since then, I've been making sure my focus and decisions have aligned with this vision. Part of that had me creating three north star goals:

1. Leverage data and technology to flip healthcare on its head.
2. Move the needle on leveling the playing field.
3. Not raise asshole kids.

What's not included here are some more personal dreams, like living in France for part of the year or going to Bali to celebrate my fiftieth birthday. Despite the Necker Island lesson, I'm still hesitant to put these things into the universe. What if I don't do them? Will I have failed?

I've decided it's better to put them out into the universe and send some energy in the direction of these dreams. Then the opportunities might appear, and my dreams might come true. If I don't put them out there, how will I remember to make them a reality?

How will others know to help me manifest them?

VISION BOARDS

While living in the dorms of Fresno State, I watched my friend Vivian create a vision board. She made one at least once a year, sometimes twice, in the fifteen years we knew each other.

She would spend hours cutting pictures from magazines and gluing them to a board. Snippets of words, torn-out pages, and rejected pictures were scattered around her as she worked through the images to represent what she wanted. She hung the finished product in a prominent place in her dorm room, apartment, and eventually, her house. She told me she looked at the board at least once a day to remind herself of her dreams and goals. You know what?

She manifested those dreams.

She worked hard and kept her eye on her targets. I always admired her grit, determination, and focus.

A gal I used to run with did the same thing. She would tell me about her annual vision-board get-togethers as we ran along the Bay. I was curious about the process, but not curious enough to ask to be included.

One year she aimed to pay off the debt they'd incurred while her husband had been without a job. I think she had it paid off by October of that same year. She set sales goals for her business and hit them by September. These weren't easy targets—they were stretch goals.

Still, I wasn't ready to create my own, largely because I'd been afraid of failing to achieve what I put on the board. I didn't consider the positive effects of creating a vision board.

Two years ago, I created a plan for the year. Jacqueline and I went to the beach to clear our heads, then headed to a local wine bar. It was the middle of the day, so we spread out across a few of the unoccupied tables and got to work.

We didn't create vision boards, but we did map out what we wanted for the year, broken down by quarter. I resisted creating a vision board the entire time. It wasn't until the following year when we were doing another planning session that I realized I had lost the plan. I couldn't *see* how I'd done for the year.

The lesson was clear: putting goals into the world isn't enough. We have to revisit them on a regular—if not daily—basis. That way, we make sure we focus our energy and attention on what we want to manifest.

Author Tina Naughton Powers says, "Vision boards can provide us with a blueprint that aligns our desires with reality. Through the images and words we choose, we become inspired to move forward with ideas for the future we might never have considered before."

I get it now.

Recently, Jacqueline and I spent an afternoon surrounded by magazines, glue sticks, snippets of words, and cutout images. We listened to Pandora's French Café station as we cut and glued. I love the result, and it wasn't as hard as I expected. My board is a visual representation of what I want to manifest in my life. It's now hanging on the back of my office door so I can look at it daily and be inspired to go after my dreams.

LIMITED RESOURCES

A friend of mine, Lela Agrama, shared her dream to be an ornamental horticulturist.

She said, "I do feel that need to break out of the box, yet feel trapped. If I had the financial means and the desire to go back to school again, I would definitely take a huge leap. However, that's not where I am, so right now, I dream and create in my own small space.

"I'm keeping the vision alive. I realized that I can retire from teaching when I'm not super old, maybe at age fifty-eight or sixty-three. Kind of a huge difference in monthly take-home, so realistically sixty-three, but it's nice knowing I can jump ship at fifty-eight if I start to really come undone. Then I can go work somewhere that makes me happy, like a nursery, even if it is for minimum wage. I could use that money for my *midlife crisis* car that I totally want: Camaro or Dodge Charger. Haven't decided yet."

Despite being bound by obligations—both financial and familial—she is still keeping an eye on her dreams. Or at least her dream job and car.

Even in midlife, it's not too late for us to dream. We can let go of practicality and set our imaginations free to go wild. We don't have to be achievement-oriented with all of our dreams. In fact, that mindset can limit our possibilities.

It's perfectly acceptable to have a conversation, alone or with others, that starts with *what if*.

And then, write it down or create a collage of pictures, and share it with a dream enabler or two.

WHAT IS DREAMING IN MIDLIFE?

Most of the women I spoke with were determined to achieve something important in their lives. They each viewed *something important* in radically different ways.

- Amy wanted to solve a problem that she suffered from and created a product and a company.
- Dorothy wanted to live and create art in France and made it happen.
- Susan started *Waggit* because she wanted to leave the world a better place for animals. It wasn't a matter of *one day*; it was now.
- Katie did some exploring and realized she wanted greater fulfillment in her life. She's gone back to school to become a marriage and family counselor.
- Connie wanted to help more highly sensitive people than she could in her own practice, so she wrote and published her first book.
- Eileen wanted to help refugees, so she took steps and is now working with the United Nations and the International Refugee Committee.
- Jeanne struggled with her menopause transition journey and didn't want other women to have the same terrible experience. She launched a company to share her research and provide women with solutions.

- Alicia saw that women founders didn't know how to get funded and launched *Women Get Funded* to educate women around the world.
- Carliza knows the value of teeth and gum health and wants to make sure that all can get access to good dental care, even in remote villages.
- Debbie wants to be a screenwriter so she can write from her lived experience. She's pursuing an advanced English degree to make this a reality.

This is the common theme for women in midlife. There is a sense that now is the time to pursue the dream. It's no longer about being our aspirational selves; it's all about leveraging our experience, who we are now, and not saying *someday.*

It's about making it happen.

Someday is *now.*

DO I NEED A WISH LIST?

Yes! We all need a wish list.

We need something to keep reaching for, even if we think it may be completely beyond our grasp. In midlife, we are nowhere close to being done.

My kids went to a summer camp where they talked to them about filters. How putting an idea or wish or dream or vision out into the world—and saying it out loud—makes you look at the world a little differently.

It's kind of like when you get a red car, all of a sudden, all you see are red cars. Or if you are pregnant or want to be pregnant, all you see are pregnant women and babies and strollers and other accoutrements.

It gets to a point where you can't *not* see these things.

But first, you have to have the courage to put the ideas out into the world and write down your wish list. When I finally told my husband I wanted to fly helicopters, all I saw were helicopters. I wasn't ready to do anything about it until my husband gave me a discovery flight for my thirty-eighth birthday.

Would I have pursued the dream of flying if I hadn't told my husband? I'm not sure. But having it on my virtual wish list gave me the courage to share my dream with him. I will be forever grateful that my husband was stupid enough to help me cross that one off the list by giving me the gift of flight for my birthday!

MY WISH LIST

- Writing and publishing this book
- Getting into better shape by the time I turn fifty
- Writing my next book
- Going to Bali for a yoga retreat after I turn fifty to celebrate turning fifty
- Becoming a paid speaker on international stages
- Living part of every year in France
- Traveling around Japan
- Learning how to bartend (or just make great cocktails)
- Visiting Cuba
- Speaking French fluently
- Taking cooking classes at the Cordon Bleu at various locations around the world
- Being the go-to expert witness for life sciences / SaaS litigation
- Visiting every major league ballpark in North America

Wow! This is kind of fun . . .

Taking the Controls

— What's on my wish list?
— What is one thing I can do this week to make my dream come true?
— What can I do next week?

BRIEFING NOTES

PARIS IS ALWAYS A GOOD IDEA

At the beginning of the year, I started meditating, stretching, and breathing every morning. When I miss a day or two, I feel the difference. When I meditate, I feel more at ease and better able to weather the storms that pop up in my life.

About the time I started meditating, I learned about Julia Cameron's *morning pages*. Every morning, as I enjoy my cup of coffee at the counter in the kitchen, I write three handwritten pages of whatever comes to mind. If I can't think of anything to write, I write about the weather, what the kids and my husband are doing, and where the animals are in the house. If I have an issue, I try to work it out as I write. It's liberating. I try not to miss a day, even if the morning pages end up being evening pages.

One night, I was talking to my husband about going to France. Between this book, my son graduating from high school, and other work demands, I didn't think I could pull it off. He said, "Why don't you use the trip as a reward for reaching a goal with the book? You've worked hard, and you deserve it. You know how much you love France."

That night I'd had enough wine to say, "Screw it!" and sent a note to my friend Terry in Paris, asking if I could stay with her. She responded, "Of course! Can't wait to see you. When will you be here?"

I looked online for airline tickets and couldn't find a reasonably priced business-class ticket. My husband said, "It's Paris . . . just book the damn economy ticket!"

Morning came, the wine buzz was gone, and reality set in. I came up with nine reasons why it would be ridiculous for me to go, including:

1. It's too expensive.
2. I'll be away from the family.

3. My family needs me.
4. What if I miss something back home?
5. Do I really need to see Paris again?
6. How could I go to France again and not bring Rei?
7. I should be focusing on client work.
8. I don't have anything to wear. Nothing fits.
9. What if there's an emergency?

To stop my head from spinning, I rolled out my yoga mat, found a Simple Habit meditation for anxiety, pressed the Breathe button on my Apple Watch, and fell into child's pose.

Once my brain was calm, I spent twenty minutes writing about it in my morning pages. Damned if I didn't have a clearer head and better perspective.

I concluded that this year would be a great year to fly to a different part of France, rent a car, and explore on my own. I didn't have to fly business class; I could fly economy plus and still get overhead space. I could find a way to sleep on the plane instead of watching back-to-back episodes of *Silicon Valley*. With the right plan, I would show up refreshed, confident, and ready to explore.

It's only money. I've made it before, and I can make it again. My family won't even notice I am gone. They'll be happy to have dinner at the counter every night rather than at the table with candles and linen napkins. My husband won't have to make the bed every morning. The dog might miss me, but she can barely handle it when I leave to run an errand, so what are two weeks?

All things French are on my vision board, so I'm putting my wish to visit France out into the universe so she can work her magic.

Chapter 10

WILD BLUE YONDER:
EXPLORATION AND EXPERIMENTATION

What if everything we thought to be true wasn't?

What if we stopped assuming that we already knew we would be good at something, or like something, or hate something?

Imagine the opportunities that would open up and the things we could learn that might lead to something else even more wonderful and interesting.

Midlife is the best time to adopt a beginner mindset in terms of exploring and experimenting. Imagine suiting up as an explorer or putting on a lab coat. Running experiments as you take steps in new directions. Testing out new things with the objective to learn and grow. Imagine the freedom! Imagine knowing and believing there is no failure—only the quest for knowledge.

Some of us who are goal-oriented may need to reframe experimentation in our minds; it can be a productive act.

There is no pass or fail.

There is only the opportunity to learn.

We're expected to follow our passions, or so society says. But what if we don't know what we're passionate about?

The authors of the book *Designing Your Life* found that many people are unable to develop a passion for something until it becomes familiar. To become familiar with something, we have to try it. That is sometimes the tricky part.

As a teenager, I hated sushi. I wasn't picky at the time and still can't believe I didn't like it. When I finally tried it ten years later, however, I couldn't (and still can't) get enough of it. I also hated hummus for years but tried it and developed an obsession with it when I was pregnant with my daughter. Now, I eat it almost every day.

As we explore, we can listen to our intuition. Pay attention. Get past the fear, trepidation, skepticism, and cynicism, and don't ignore the feelings. Everything we do gets us to a new place.

Bev and I discussed my writing experience one day, causing her to share her memoir-writing process. She said, "I may write entire chapters or sections and then throw them away. But what I end up writing and keeping couldn't have existed without the previous work."

Still not convinced?

Read on.

RIGHT TIMING

After twenty years in tech, Amy knew it was time to look for something new.

She said, "Five years ago, I had no trouble finding a new tech job. Then I spent a year job hunting and interviewing and couldn't find a new job. I kept getting feedback that I wasn't enough of this or that. I thought I might have aged out of tech at forty-five. It felt as if the bar kept moving, and it was exhausting. My ego took a huge blow.

"I started taking art classes and was helping the owner with her marketing. One day, she asked me to teach something to the kids in the studio. I didn't have any experience but said *yes* anyway. I don't remember what I was teaching, but they became engaged very quickly, and I thought, *What about teaching? Could I be a teacher?* I'd never thought about it before."

She asked a few friends about their experience as teachers and was told, "There will be a teacher shortage, but you might want to look into something other than art, because art classes are the first thing to be eliminated with budget cuts."

"I talked to my mother-in-law," Amy said. "She was a teacher and suggested that I observe a few teachers in action. I visited some classrooms and saw a variety of teaching styles. One of the first teachers I talked to said that being a teacher is like being the CEO of your own classroom."

The more teachers she watched, the more this made sense.

After a year, she had her teaching credentials and quickly had her own classroom. She loves it. She can put into practice her years of experience working with people and her early college education in psychology, and feels as if it's all come together as it should have.

It all started with exploring an art class.

EXPLORE. GET LOST. BRING SNACKS.

I love going on little road trips with my kids, but especially with my daughter, Rei.

On one of our last trips, Rei and I packed overnight bags, got in the car, and started driving. I gave her A/B choices that eventually took us down the coast. It was a cold but beautiful day. While we enjoyed the view of the Pacific Ocean, I decided to head into the Santa Cruz mountains.

We were chatting, listening to music, appreciating the beautiful scenery, and watching the ever-changing weather that alternated between sunshine and rain. Fortunately, Rei brought chocolate kisses because it started to feel like Gilligan's three-hour tour. Hunger soon set in.

At one point while we were completely lost, I pulled over and stepped into the trees to feel nature and snap a few pics. Even though we were about forty-five minutes from home, it felt so much further away. Except for the birds and the bugs, the trees were silent and so serene. It was just what I needed.

We eventually hit Highway 9, found a roadside restaurant, and had a late lunch. Well-fed, we hopped back into the car and headed toward Santa Cruz instead of to our favorite, well-known hotel in San Francisco.

Wrong choice.

Within minutes of arriving in our room, we discovered ourselves in a poorly placed situation with an elevator-noise problem. A loud one. To make matters worse, the noisy heater barely covered the obnoxious sounds from the hall. Uncharacteristically, I called down to the front desk and asked for a new room. When they said they didn't have any available, I called their booking office and asked for help. Then a refund. When they offered a credit, I politely asked for (OK, maybe not *so* politely) a refund.

They gave it.

We ended up driving home rather than enduring a difficult night. I could have seen it as a failed exploration, but it wasn't. Rei and I have shared memories that we can laugh over—really, they weren't painful or traumatic—and we have a new plan.

1. Choose a direction, and then do the opposite.
2. If we're debating between a new hotel and Hotel Zetta in San Francisco, we choose Hotel Zetta.

Exploring in midlife isn't much different.

If we take time to learn from the experience and relish the victories, it's not failure.

My victory, besides time with Rei, was in asking for what I wanted. Often, I don't because I hate to be seen as difficult. This time I did, and everything worked out.

The midlife journey is not a straight path. It's circuitous, with switchbacks and double backs. But, in the end, it's definitely worth the effort and discomfort of exploring, especially with fun people and good snacks.

CHANGING YOUR MIND ISN'T FAILURE

When I returned from Necker Island the first time, I wanted to start thinking bigger. I knew I could execute someone else's vision, but could I create my own?

I wanted to think bigger, but I had no idea how to do it on my own. That's when I hired Julie Gordon White.

We worked for three months to create my big vision. I loved angel investing but had limited capital to work with. I decided to raise money from other investors and create a new venture fund to invest in startups with products and services for the rest of us, not just what pattern-matched or resonated with primarily white, male venture capitalists (VCs).

I created an investment thesis, drafted a pitch deck, purchased the necessary domains, created an LLC, and socialized the idea a little bit. I even managed to get up the courage to ask a few folks to invest in the fund. A few surprising yesses, and some more surprising and disappointing noes, came through.

At the time, my heart wasn't 100% in it. I couldn't figure out the problem. Was I scared?

Turned out to be something else.

At a women's conference later that year, I learned about ways to achieve my goal of making it easier for women to get access to capital, but I didn't have to go the VC route to do it. The VC path never felt *quite* right because it wasn't aligning with my values.

I shelved the VC fund idea and created a global mesh network of like-minded investors. It's informal, less risky, and connects female investors who would not have otherwise connected. Best of all, I don't have to commit 100% of my time to only one thing. I like variety.

This wasn't failure; this was exploration, learning, and adapting.

GETTING STARTED

If you're like me, you might have a million things you're interested in exploring, but not enough time. Or you may be like Lindsay and have no idea where to start. Or maybe you're like Lisa and feel paralyzed by all the options.

Where you are is where you are.

No judgment.

Here's a little exercise to get you started. If you don't know where to start, begin by creating a list of things you love and/or used to love. Get out a piece of paper and a writing implement, or open up your computer or the Notes app on your phone, and start listing things you would consider trying, want to try, or will try.

No self-judgment. No limits.

This is not a spelling test, and you won't be graded, so don't hold back. This doesn't have to be done in one sitting, either. You can start the list and keep adding to it. If you're totally stuck on this exercise, there are various things you can do to get unstuck.

- Pull up past memories. In Julia Cameron's book, *It's Never Too Late to Begin Again,* she has the reader go through a memoir exercise each week that can help trigger ideas through memories. There might have been something you really liked to do earlier in your life and wanted to pursue, but someone talked you out of it. (Might have been you!) Or life got in the way, and you stopped doing it. Now might be the perfect time to revisit.

- Buy *The Artist's Way.* My friend Ann followed the twelve-week program in that book to explore her interests. She found it to be a very helpful program. My friend Gaby has done that same program and periodically repeats it as well. This may be a solid option for you.

- Read *Designing Your Life* to get ideas on how to explore.

- Roam a bookstore. Julie had me spend an hour in a bookstore wandering around, taking pictures of covers that caught my eye. Then we reviewed them to see if there were any patterns. The last ones I took, ironically enough, were all in the art section.

- Talk to other people. Ask them what they do for work or in their spare time or what they like to read, listen to, or watch. Be curious, and see what comes up.
- If you don't like talking to other people, look at Pinterest, browse social media, listen to podcasts, watch YouTube videos, or take an online class. You never know where something interesting might come from.
- Ask yourself questions. *What do I love,* or *what do I hate?* is a great place to start. *What do I want to look back on and be proud of?* Or even, *Is there anything that I will look back on and regret not having done?*

Once you have some semblance of a list, see what jumps out at you. What might be the easiest to get started on? Take some action to check it out.

It's really that simple.

No need to sign up for year-long classes or escape to Madagascar. The first step could be as simple as an internet search, reading a book, taking one class, or downloading a new app. Remove the reasons why it's impossible, and think more along the lines of, *what if . . .*

No more limiting beliefs.

As you try on new things, check in with yourself. See how you feel. Reflect on the experiences.

What did you like?

What did you learn?

What do you want more of?

What do you want to avoid forevermore?

Do you want to keep exploring or try something different?

Carve out time for this in your schedule, and make it a priority. Once you get started doing it and gain some momentum, it may just become part of who you are.

Don't Box Me In

As we explore, avoid pigeonholing or labeling. It's limiting. Now is the time to be expansive.

Others may want to chime in and label you, but don't listen to them. It might help them simplify their world, but it shouldn't narrow yours.

A few years ago, I had issues with a guy who decided that I needed to fit into a certain box. It was his box, not my box. Let's call him John. I'd been asked to be the CTO (chief technology officer) for a startup. Flattered, I considered it for about a minute. I told John (who I thought was my friend) about the opportunity.

He said, "You aren't CTO material. It's really challenging to deal with the technical staff and contractors. You can't do that."

After I picked my jaw up off the floor, I asked if he knew what I did for a living. This was exactly what I did every damn day.

A few months later, I think I'd invited him to dinner and mentioned that I was going to be cooking, probably something French from Julia Child.

"You don't cook," he said. "Do you even know how?"

What?

While my husband does most of the daily cooking because that's his job as the stay-at-home parent, I love to cook but rarely have time. And I'm pretty good at it. Unfortunately, I hear this kind of thing all the time.

"You don't look like an angel investor."

"You don't look like a helicopter pilot."

"You can't do that; you're a girl."

People like to put us in categories that make sense for *them*. It makes their lives easier. In midlife, as we're exploring, experimenting, and redefining, we have to let go of their expectations and limitations and say, "Don't box me in!"

LEARN AS YOU GO

I may sound like a broken record at this point, but this is an important point. Experimenting and exploring are opportunities to test things out, try new things, or try old things from a different angle. Some things are going to work, and other things are not. Both are opportunities to learn.

If you feel as if you've made a mistake, forgive yourself. See the mistake as a gift to grow from.

The goal is to learn, not to be right or wrong. In fact—there is no right or wrong. There are no blue ribbons or gold stars handed out. Unless you decide to award them to yourself for trying new things. In that case, fill up that damn sticker chart!

This is a time to be curious and open. Listen to yourself, and follow your instincts, too. Feel a tug in your soul? Follow it. All of this will lead to new learning, meeting new people, and learning about what you love, what you like, and what you want to avoid.

Another thing to consider—find what feels right, and see what fits into your lifestyle, too.

STRETCHING

When I worked for my dad, we would argue about tax law.

He would remind me that there is black on one side of the spectrum and white on the other. The gray area in between was our playground. I saw things pretty clearly as right or wrong, black or white. He encouraged me to expand the gray area. Eventually, I would. I'd stretch like a rubber band and inevitably snap right back to narrow the gray area.

You know what, though? I never went back to the same binary place of right/wrong. Each time I expanded my thinking, I increased the gray area in between.

This is what happens when we try new things through experimentation or exploration. We are never the same again.

We've gained new experiences, new memories, new skills, and oftentimes new people, and are forever changed. We've changed our vantage point, which means we just might be able to see things we couldn't see before.

BRING A FRIEND

Julia Cameron encourages her readers to go on solo artist dates to build a better relationship with themselves.

These artist dates are designed for us to explore something new and see what comes up. If you aren't a solo explorer, find a friend. What if they're stuck, too, and need some help to try something new? Drag them along on your adventures, and encourage them to experiment.

Just make sure that your analysis and assessments are your own. This isn't the time to be asking for someone else's opinion.

As for my solo adventures, maybe I need an imaginary friend.

TAKING THE CONTROLS

— What have I always wanted to try?
— What can I do now to make it a reality?
— What would I do if I knew I couldn't fail?

BRIEFING NOTES

CHAPTER 11

THE PATH WILL
PRESENT ITSELF

When I became an angel investor, I wanted to learn as much as I could, as quickly as possible.

I attended events, read articles and books, talked to other investors, and listened to podcasts. It became very clear to me very quickly that angel investing was the white bro show. There weren't women like me—in fact, there weren't very many women at all. There weren't people of color. The lack of diversity made me think, *I can't be the only one who doesn't feel represented.*

I decided to launch a podcast to give voice to more people and provide inspiration to the rest of us. I launched the podcast *Piloting Your Life* in September 2017. I'd like to say it was a complete success—but I would be lying.

While I became better at interviews and messaging, I completely missed targeting a consistent audience. I tried to be something for a broad group of listeners, which was exactly the wrong thing to do. I'd look at the download numbers with my producer, Jacqueline, and feel devastated. My friends weren't even listening. They'd say, "Sorry, I don't listen to podcasts," or "Sorry, I'm completely behind on podcast episodes."

My husband and mother weren't even listening!

When I felt like a complete failure and contemplated quitting, I would stop, talk myself off the ledge, and reflect on the experience. I've interviewed some amazing people, shared their stories, shared *my* stories, engaged with new people, and created content that wouldn't otherwise be out there. When someone asks me for advice about a certain topic, chances are I've done an episode about it, and I can send them the link.

And I gave a voice to people who wouldn't otherwise have been heard.

Why did I keep going if I thought no one was listening? Because I knew that if I kept on doing it, eventually I would land on the right thing. I wouldn't have been able to get there if I didn't start. While I felt the first year was a bomb (not da bomb), I learned to be more specific, and I used my platform to expand on topics that interested me.

I used my platform for advocacy and education and released my hundredth episode in April 2019.

Four years ago, if someone would have said that I would have a podcast, I would have said they were crazy. If they'd said I would be using a platform like this to advocate for women, I would have thought they were insane.

Me?

Really?

Yep. Really.

I often wondered, *Why the hell am I doing this if no one is listening?* It takes dedication, effort, time, and money to release a weekly podcast. But then, every once in a while, I would get an email or bump into someone who would comment on how much an episode meant to them. I would stop, breathe, express my thanks, and think, "Someone *is* listening."

Not only were they listening, but they took the time to write an email or say thank you. Best of all, the podcast led to this book. I've been able to refine my voice on-air, and with my weekly In-Flight newsletter, I learned how to write. And to love it.

The podcast came about in steps:

1. Starting with an idea
2. Hiring Jacqueline as my producer
3. Refining the concept
4. Creating the cover art

5. Recording the first interviews
6. Setting up the tech, website, and distribution platform

Without that first step, I wouldn't be where I am today. Of course, at the time, I couldn't see where this was going. I felt as if I were meandering down the path, but I chose to have faith in the process and took the first step.

For the last four years, my mantra has been: *the path will present itself.* If something isn't working, I dig in and ask, *Why isn't it working?* Then I take action, even if it's small, to change things up. I now see life as a series of experiments, with failure only being a failure of reflection and learning.

New paths and opportunities have opened up as a result.

This is what midlife is all about: take the first step, then the next, and then see what comes from it. Explore with curiosity. Stop to reflect. Figure out the next step. Sometimes the path needs to unfold. (It would be great to have a red carpet, though!)

Not sure where the next opportunity will come from? Get out, and meet new people. Talk about new things. Explore new avenues, and see what pops up. Take a class. Go to a meet-up.

Your next opportunity will most likely come from something unexpected.

CHANCE MEETINGS, UNEXPECTED OPPORTUNITIES

I met Tawana in the Frankfurt Lufthansa lounge in February 2017.

I'd just gotten off an eleven-hour flight from San Francisco and had seven hours to kill before my next flight to Toulouse, France. As usual, I hadn't slept well on the flight and felt grungy and out of sorts. A corner of the lounge beckoned me, so I set up camp. It would have been the furthest corner, but Tawana got there first.

I don't even remember what got us talking. Maybe it was because actress Rene Russo sat across from us at one point. After she left, I know we looked at each other and asked, almost at the same time, "Was that Rene Russo?"

It definitely was.

Tawana and I started with the typical questions. I must have complained about my crazy schedule and trying to find balance because she said, "I started meditating, and it's been a game changer for me. I try to meditate daily, even if it's just for five minutes."

I'd been pretty skeptical about meditation and said, "I can't sit still long enough to meditate." (I'd used the same excuse for yoga.) But here was a successful woman, a global traveler, and she meditated. She didn't fit the image of the *meditation person* I had in my head. The timing must have been right—and I must have been ready to hear it—because I downloaded the app.

Then my turn came to share. I spoke about my journey into angel investing (sounds like I am trying to convert someone to a religion), about the importance of supporting underrepresented founders, and getting more women to start investing. Fascinated, she wanted to learn more. I encouraged her to look into local opportunities when she returned to New Jersey.

The seven hours flew by. We parted ways in the terminal as she headed to Barcelona and I headed to Toulouse.

We kept in touch and met up in Silicon Valley when she was visiting the Facebook mother ship. During one visit, we went on a walk near Stanford University. As we walked through the crisp fall air, among the variegated trees, we chatted again about angel investing.

She said, "Our conversation about angel investing really stuck with me. I think I'm ready to take a closer look."

"Check out Pipeline Angels," I said.

Within a year, she had joined the group and invested in nine startups. She'd gotten involved in Startup Newark in Newark, New Jersey and Digital Undivided in Atlanta, Georgia. She was recently interviewed at the New York Stock Exchange and talked about her involvement with Pipeline Angels and how female investors are helping female entrepreneurs.

"When I joined Pipeline Angels and walked into the first meeting," she said, "I saw people like me. There were black and brown-skinned women. I wanted this to become the norm, not the exception. I am now actively encouraging other women like me to get into investing. I am encouraging other female investors to support and invest in female founders, especially black and brown founders."

She recently sent me the following text: "I would not have done it had I known what it really was, but you make a good point about discomfort when you referred to how messy and uncomfortable the writing process has been for you."

Two things on this:

1. You never know what you'll learn from someone you talk to in an airport when you are sitting across from a celebrity.
2. Sometimes doing something new is uncomfortable.

We need to move through our discomfort and trust in the goodness on the other side. We need to trust that when we take a step, the next step will be more obvious.

Two more things:

1. It helps to get encouragement from others when forging a new path.
2. It's all about putting one foot in front of the other.

REFLECTION AND REDIRECTION

When we explore and put faith into experimentation, we trust that we're taking the necessary steps. For this to be effective, we must pause, reflect, note our learnings, and celebrate our victories.

Otherwise, we may miss something important or think we've wasted our time. As Bev says, "Nothing is ever wasted. There is always something to be learned."

We can choose a new way of thinking that encourages self-awareness, self-improvement, and empowerment. These work when we shift our attention from the never-ending to-do list and ask:

- What went well?
- What did I learn?
- What could be done differently?
- What resources do I need to move forward?

As a project manager, I've been trained to perform project debriefs at the end of every project. The goal is to gather helpful insights and information to improve future projects within the organization.

I gather the team members into a room and ask them the following questions:

- Did we achieve our objectives?
- What went well?
- What could we have done differently?
- What did you learn/gain from the project?

The projects I work on are technology projects, but the methodology can be applied to any project. I remember doing this exercise when I was twenty years old and a member of the local Junior Chamber of Commerce (Jaycee) chapter.

We ran events in our community and documented all that we planned to do and what we did, including the outcomes. I was the project lead on the annual Easter egg hunt for underprivileged kids in Hayward, California. I put the plan together, submitted it to the board, received approval, recruited sponsors, and had 50-100 kids show up. I even convinced my sister to dress up as the Easter bunny. After the event, we met together, performed the debrief, and assessed the project. This became part of the documentation, and the next year we were able to make the event even better.

Not everyone wants to do this. I've managed client projects where the project team and company leadership just didn't see the value. The team members resisted the exercise, thinking it a waste of time to dwell on what was already done. This feels short-sighted to me.

Midlife isn't the time for being short-sighted.

Last fall, I went back through my calendar and detailed, by month, everything I'd accomplished throughout the year. I'd been so focused and overwhelmed by what I wanted to do that I'd forgotten what I'd actually done. I hadn't stopped to celebrate any wins or reflect on my accomplishments; I'd just powered through.

Once I went through the exercise, I realized I could see the path—the logical progression—but only in hindsight. I thought, "Holy hell! I am a badass."

Søren Kierkegaard said, "Life can only be understood backwards; but it must be lived forwards."

Celebrate the Wins

Admittedly, I'm terrible about celebrating my victories.

I didn't feel victorious when I released episode 100 of my podcast. Most podcasts don't get past seven episodes, so 100 is quite an accomplishment. In my mind, I constantly think, "That's great, whatever. But what are you going to do next?"

This kind of thinking is deeply flawed.

My producer Jacqueline also struggles. To help her out, I've started to point out when something has gone well for her or she's successfully made it through something tough. I remind her of her accomplishment so she can remember to pat herself on the back for a job well done. She does the same for me.

It's a step in the right direction.

Don't be afraid to crack open the mental champagne (or some

actual champagne) to celebrate the victories. Pat yourself on the back for a job well done, then put the lessons to work.

SHIFTING ENERGY

Once we start making decisions, we realize we can make more and bigger decisions. It gets easier over time, and our energy starts to shift.

It's all about building up the *change* muscle.

Marina was in her late forties when she started to reclaim her life. She said, "I didn't really realize it was happening at the time, but it makes sense when I look back. My son was born prematurely, and we almost lost him at five weeks. I held my breath for the first two years. I thought we'd gotten lucky and didn't want to rock the boat. I chose to just be grateful and let go of everything else."

As she stepped more into herself, she said, "My marriage started to fall apart. I now see that it needed to happen for me to fully claim my life and myself. Then I just needed to keep going because my marriage had failed."

She tried to do the work on her own but realized she couldn't. "I was really struggling and in a lot of pain," she said. "One day while I was working at home, I'd had enough. I said, 'Fuck it,' grabbed my computer, and started watching some videos of a coach I knew. I hired him to help me, and that's when everything shifted."

This was one of the first times she chose herself and made herself a priority—it's made all the difference.

"I've been meditating. And with the work I've been doing with my coach, I've been able to process things in brand-new ways. It's making the divorce easier, and I can be there for my son too. I am more in tune with my intuition. My coach has taught me to listen to my inner voice. I used to be highly intuitive, but that voice became muffled, and I lost my ability to hear it. It's back now."

As she gains clarity on what she wants and needs, new professional and personal opportunities are opening up in unexpected ways.

"There's so much going on right now. A few new job options have opened up, and I'm exploring writing a book. I might train others on breath work. It was so impactful for me that I want others to experience the energy shift and joy I've discovered. I am so grateful."

She's beginning to dream again.

She continues to do the work and take the steps that are leading to bigger and more fulfilling things in her life. She said, "I am changing, and I know it's for the better. I know there's no going back."

The energy has shifted.

That place no longer exists.

SETTING AN EXAMPLE

My friend Xandra retired from her corporate job to stay home with her kids over a decade ago.

"As they got older," she said, "I wanted them to see me doing something for myself and something that makes me happy."

This decision was her first step toward investing in startups, helping women invest, and advising founders with launching and scaling their businesses.

"I wanted flexibility to spend time with my kids and travel with my husband. I set that as a requirement for whatever I chose to pursue. A few opportunities came up over the years, but none of them gave me the flexibility I needed, so I passed on them."

Xandra attacked the problem the only way she knew how: through an organized and logical approach.

"I created a list of what I loved to do and started talking to people. I explored what was out there and decided to join an angel investing group. I thought this would give me access to people I could learn and grow from and help me find the next step."

During her time with the angel group, she learned about investing in startups and thought her friends could benefit. She knows the statistics around women, money, and investing and wanted to do something to change it all for the better.

"I created OSEA Angels to bring women together to learn how to invest. One thing led to another, and I was introduced into the entrepreneurial centers at the local universities and saw a chance to bring more groups together to support local founders.

"At each step of this journey, I stopped to reflect on what I was doing. I still do. I look at what is working and celebrate my wins. This is very important to me. I also strategize around my next step and what resources I am going to need to move forward."

As for her kids, Xandra said, "I keep my kids in the loop, so they know what I'm doing. I want to be a solid role model, whether they know it or not. I'm enjoying what I'm doing right now. OSEA Angels is thriving. I love educating women as investors and supporting the local founder community. I always have an eye open to new opportunities. I want to continue to have a positive impact in my community and have a great time doing it."

OPEN SESAME

As we take steps toward new opportunities, some doors may present where we couldn't see them before. Sometimes those doors may not open no matter how much we bang on them. But that's okay (or so I keep telling myself). It may not be the right time—or it might not be the right opportunity.

When I was laid off for the first time, I was thirty-two. Bev suggested I start consulting on my own. "Nope," I said. "Not ready."

But when I was laid off the second time three years later, I knew it was time to take control of my destiny.

I started to write a book when I got back from Necker Island the first time. I decided to do it and came up with a theme and a title. (*Keep a Tiara in Your Glovebox and Champagne in the Fridge . . .* I may still write that book!) I started writing. I socialized the idea with some women and realized I wasn't thinking big enough. Then I completely stalled out and set the project aside for two years until I heard my writing coach/editor, Katie, on a podcast. I knew in my soul that it was time and that she was the right person to work with.

I had to take the steps and take the chance.

Only through action and movement can we clear the path for the right opportunities.

THE PATH IS CLEAR . . . IN HINDSIGHT

After her second child was born, Jacqueline and her then-husband Adam decided that she would stay home with the kids. Her oldest daughter was almost three.

Jacqueline has a Ph.D. and worked in a research lab at Stanford University. She said, "I enjoyed my work and was sad about leaving. But I also wanted to enjoy time with my children. I wanted to be home to raise them. I chose to put my kids first, which I don't regret, but I definitely felt like I was treading water for a lot of years. While I was a full-time stay-at-home mom, I adapted to meet the needs of my kids, but didn't feel like it was fulfilling mine.

"I started working at Weight Watchers to have something that was mine. I needed and wanted flexibility to pick the kids up after school, go on field trips, and work in their classrooms."

I asked her if she looked for anything else, and she said, "No. I took the Weight Watchers opportunity because it was there."

She didn't have a bigger or grander plan. It was simply one step.

During her work at Weight Watchers, she learned that she really enjoyed the conversations around helping people work through their issues. "I liked having mini-coaching conversations. I decided to look into coaching. I took a few courses. About the same time, I asked my husband for a divorce and needed to stop dabbling. I needed to find a way to financially support myself and my girls."

She applied for a job that looked interesting, but didn't get it. She worked on expanding her coaching business and couldn't quite get it to where she wanted it, either.

At the time, I had a few projects that I needed help with and asked her if she would be open to working on them with me. Despite never having done the work before, she agreed.

"I knew there were 100 people out there 100 times more qualified than me," she said, "but I was happy to do the work and was 100% committed to producing my best. It wasn't a terribly big risk. I knew I could tell you if I didn't know how to do something. Plus, I'm good at research and figuring stuff out."

That she is.

She worked on a rebranding project where all of her skills and experience came together. Research + art + life coaching. The perfect Jacqueline combination.

She's now at a point where she's making the hard decisions about *what* to work on because her professional plate is full.

"Looking back," she said, "it looks like the stepping-stones create a clear and visible path, but I never felt like there was a clear path. I took advantage of opportunities to learn and grow; I took some chances, and I just kept moving forward."

Jacqueline's journey is by no means complete, and her next steps aren't completely clear. We can only take the steps, sometimes mustering up the courage to do so, to see what's next. Sometimes we'll double back, which is just fine as long as we've learned from the experience.

Then there's the celebration. We all need to break out the glitter and party hats and say, "Atta girl!"

TAKING THE CONTROLS

— What are three things I can do to get closer to what I want in my life?
— What recent win can I celebrate?

BRIEFING NOTES

PARIS? MAIS OUI!

A few years ago, my friend Andrea sent me a text that said, *Hey! Want to meet me in Paris and keep me company while hubby is at COP21?*

First, I had to ask what COP21 was (a big climate change conference); then I asked, *When?* She said, *We leave in six weeks.*

Without thinking, I said, *Yes.* I reached out to my friend Terry in Paris to see if I could stay at her place, and she said yes almost immediately. First problem solved. Flights were next. Seats were available on Andrea's flights, and I was even able to use miles! It all came together in about a week.

Then the second-guessing kicked in, a nagging feeling as if I were missing something. I'd left my family before, so I didn't know what was bothering me so much. As I worked through my mental anguish, I kept getting hung up when I thought about my daughter. I kept feeling as if I were missing something.

Weird.

The trip ended up being amazing. I drank too much. Ate too much. Got too little sleep. Enjoyed all of my favorite parts of Paris, including champagne at Hotel Le Meurice and lunch at L'Atelier.

On the last night, we stayed at a hotel near the airport. I had trouble sleeping and woke up at around 1:00 a.m. and checked my phone. My daughter had texted me to say that her period had started. My mama senses knew before I left for the trip that something was going to happen with her. This was a painful moment. Here I was, in France (which she loves), away from my daughter while she was experiencing a special, transitional time.

You can't imagine the guilt.

Fortunately, she had a chat thread going with her friends, who provided her with support; my husband made sure she had product, and my neighbor Lindsay made sure she had female support. I felt terrible but knew she was in good hands.

Would I have done this differently if I'd known that her period was going to start? Nope. It makes for a great story, and she was well supported. I chatted and texted with her that night, and she was all good.

How could I pass up a trip to Paris? I had a place to stay with friends. I booked flights with miles. And I had a gal pal to explore Paris with.

Sometimes we need to jump at these opportunities and see where they take us.

And Paris? *Mais oui!*

Chapter 12

TAKING RISKS

Diana Nyad first attempted to swim from Cuba to Florida when she was twenty years old. She was sixty-four when she made her fifth and final attempt, successfully completing the 110-mile swim. It took her fifty-three hours and a support team of thirty people. Why did she keep trying after so many failed attempts?

Because she didn't want to look back and have regrets.

She said, "When I turned sixty, the dream was still alive from having tried this in my twenties—dreamed it and imagined it. The most famous body of water on the Earth today, I imagine, Cuba to Florida. And it was deep. It was deep in my soul."[21]

On the day of the swim, her team told her it was impossible. She chose to go anyway, following her mantra, *find a way.*

"None of us ever get through this life without heartache, without turmoil," Nyad said. "If you believe and have faith, and you can get knocked down and get back up again, and you believe in perseverance as a great human quality, you'll find your way. Every day of our lives is epic. I'm walking around tall because I am a bold, fearless person. And I will be, every day, until it's time for these days to be done."

We can't all be like Diana Nyad. We all have different risk tolerances, hobbies, and perceptions of risk. Even so, to grow, to gain new experiences, to build new neural pathways, and to truly live our lives, we have to step outside our comfort zone and take risks. And guess what? Taking small risks helps build the muscle for taking more and bigger risks. We each only have one life to live—might as well make it a good one!

Eleanor Roosevelt said, "Do one thing every day that scares you."

In midlife, it is way too easy to be on autopilot, but it's also the worst thing we can do for our health, happiness, and longevity. Midlife is an amazing opportunity to define what we want and who we want to be in the next half of our lives.

We need to step outside our comfort zone, take risks, and claim our lives for ourselves.

CALCULATING RISK

Some of my friends look at me funny when I say that I'm not a big risk-taker.

I am a *calculated* risk-taker. That's not the same as being a *big* risk-taker. They point out my angel investing, my helicopter flying, swapping homes with French families, going to Necker Island, and don't believe me when I say I have a relatively low tolerance for risk.

While I do all of these things, I also mitigate risks.

When I fly, I always take a flight instructor. I only fly in certain weather and when I'm not sick or tired or distracted. I also only fly in the Bay Area, which is very familiar to me.

If we're uncomfortable taking risks, calculating and reasonably assessing the risks can help us muster up the courage to do something that scares us or seems overwhelming.

ASKING FOR WHAT WE WANT

A lot of us spend too much time in our heads. When we get out of them and into the real world, we often gain greater clarity. That makes it easier to take risks, both large and small.

Maggie Neale, author of *Getting More of What You Want* (a must-read for all women) gives lectures at Stanford University on negotiating. She often discusses the negative financial consequences of failing to negotiate the best compensation package, starting with our first job.

She says that, with all else being equal, if a woman fails to negotiate the salary for her first job and receives, for example, $100,000, and her male counterpart receives $107,000, she will have to work eight years longer than he does to have the same wealth at retirement. If we fail to negotiate at each opportunity throughout our careers, it's not just eight years—it's decades.

For those of us in midlife, we can't go back. We can see our own value and ask for what we want now, whether it's an increased salary, working from home, a flight upgrade, a discount, or having the housekeeper make the bed a certain way. So many of us hold back because we don't want to seem *difficult* or *demanding* or a *bitch*.

By choosing to *not* ask for what we want, we are guaranteed to not get what we want and end up unhappy and resentful.

Maggie talks about how women suffer a likeability penalty when we negotiate for compensation, so our fear about not being liked when we ask for what we want is justified. When we get past this, we'll make great strides. Otherwise, we'll never get ahead.

Every day, I give myself pep talks to ask for what I want. It's not easy, but through practice, we can stop caring about how we appear and desensitize ourselves to hearing *no*.

FEAR OF REJECTION AND ABANDONMENT

In order to live a true and authentic life, Helene made some significant and irreversible changes.

"I had to," she told me. "I was miserable. I couldn't live as I was any longer. But some people just couldn't handle the changes. Some of my biggest fears came true. Some of the people I loved either rejected or abandoned me. I think it was hardest to lose my father.

"Now that I'm living life as my true, authentic self, I have freedom I never had before. I rebuilt relationships and created new, richer relationships. I've never been happier."

Not everyone is going to come with us when we make changes. We can be conscious of our impact, but we can't be distracted by the needs of others.

Ultimately, it's up to them to decide whether they want to change too.

FOCUS ON THE UPSIDE

It hasn't been easy for Helene, but she has newfound freedom to create and live her true life. She said, "Once you take a big risk, it's easier to not be paralyzed by fear."

Once we get past that fear paralysis, we're free to explore, learn new things, and move on to bigger and better things.

But not everything has to be a big risk.

Sometimes, sending an email to the CEO of a big company gets my heart pounding. What if they don't answer? What if they think what I wrote is ridiculous?

But . . . what if they *do* respond?

We become so focused on the negative outcomes that we often lose sight of the upside. What if we reframe the fear? Instead of saying, "What if it goes wrong?" we can say, "What if it goes right?" Focusing on the positive requires intention, and with it comes an energy shift.

When I learned how to ride a motorcycle, I was taught to focus on where I wanted to go and not on the thing I wanted to avoid, whether it was a pothole, debris, vehicle, or stray dog.

Where you look is where you go.

For those of us who can be overly concerned by what could go wrong, we could instead focus on the result we *want*, thereby increasing our odds for positive outcomes.

ROCK BOTTOM

Susanne (first introduced in chapter three) had lost her confidence and self-esteem. She didn't even know if she could pay her mortgage when she was invited to go to Necker Island, but she followed her intuition and said, "Yes."

"It was a very last-minute decision, and I wasn't sure if I was going to be able to pull it off," she said. "I'm so glad I did because it was the beginning of big and positive changes in my life. At dinner one night, Richard [Branson] said that he'd never been afraid of failing publicly. I couldn't stop thinking about this until I realized that I'd been avoiding failing publicly my entire life. That's when something clicked, and I decided I didn't need to be afraid.

"I continued to reflect on this. I knew I had been loved. I knew that I was somebody. I knew I deserved good things. When I would start to wonder if something was possible, I would say to myself, *I don't know if this is going to work, but I'm going to do it anyway.*"

Seeing what was possible for others made her realize that it was possible for her too. "I knew I was going to have to be a champion for myself in a whole new way. In a way I hadn't done before. I looked for one good professional win every day. If I didn't have one, I kept working until I had something good."

Occasionally, she would catch herself reading LinkedIn profiles and feel like she was falling behind. She even thought she needed to get a job and sell her soul to pay her mortgage.

"Then I remembered that I deserved good things, and I didn't have to compromise," she said. "On the way home from an interview, I told my husband I wasn't going to take the job. I knew I was good at my work, and I wanted to keep doing it. I was going to die trying to make it work. I shifted my mindset to *it will happen* and went for it knowing there was no backup plan."

This was when everything changed.

When she let go of the outcomes and expectations, the money and the opportunities showed up in abundance.

"It's funny. I did exactly what I encourage my clients to do. I encourage them to let go, aim to show up, and do the good work."

She took the risk, did the hard work, believed in herself, and it worked.

NOT FEELING BOLD AND GOING FOR IT ANYWAY

My favorite flight instructor is always Paul.

When I first started flying with Paul, he was a bit uptight. He's a British accountant by day and has always been very kind and supportive, which isn't the norm for helicopter flight instructors. I spent a lot of time with Paul as I built up my hours and knowledge for my commercial rating, which has greater requirements and tighter standards than the private rating. He encourages me to fly beyond my comfort zone, which I tend to resist.

A childhood friend, Lesly, sent me a note and asked if I would take her mom, June, flying for her eightieth birthday. Lesly said, "Flying in a helicopter is on my mom's bucket list, and I know she would love to check it off with you as the pilot."

After spending a few months aligning schedules, we lucked out with the weather and had a perfect day to fly. I flew her over her house in Castro Valley, California (where I grew up) and out over the green hills in the canyon. It was a gorgeous day to fly, and the conditions were perfect for a pinnacle landing, which Paul suggested.

My immediate response was, "Thank you, but no."

He'd chosen a spot on top of a hill that wasn't very challenging as far as pinnacles go. The winds were calm, and the landing spot seemed clear of cows. But I wasn't feeling very daring that day. I hadn't flown in a while and was still focusing on the basics of keeping us safe in the air.

He said, "You've got this, Terri. And, June, Terri is a really good pilot and clearly capable of doing this despite her misgivings."

That little boost gave me the extra courage to get over my trepidation. I went for it.

I flew in too high from the west and had an unexpected tailwind that introduced unacceptable risk, so I aborted the first attempt. After that, I pulled power to gain altitude, spun us around, and set us up for the perfect landing from the east. June saw a picnic table next to the spot and said, "I should have brought us a picnic lunch!"

Do you remember the scene from *National Lampoon's Vacation* where the Griswold family finally arrived at the Grand Canyon? After all their hijinks getting there, they spent a whopping five to ten seconds appreciating the view before getting back into the car and heading off to some new disastrous, but hilarious, situation.

Well, that's about the length of time I was comfortable hovering over the very dry grass.

I said, "Well, that's enough of that." I tipped the nose of the helicopter, pulled some power, and flew from the spot, breathing a major sigh of relief.

Paul had more confidence in me than I did. Not five minutes later, he said to me, "Why don't you do a hover at altitude so we can watch that fire over there in the canyon?"

WTF, Paul?

I'd barely started breathing normally from the pinnacle landing. My hands were still sweaty! Now he wanted me to push my limits once again. So, I bled off the airspeed to get to zero and hung out at 800 feet doing what airplanes can't do . . . hovering. Then I spun us around to get the full panoramic view of the area.

The view was stunning. We'd had quite a bit of rain, and all we could see were the verdant, green hills.

Then it was time to go. Once again, I pulled power, tilted the nose, and headed back to the airport with sweaty hands and shaking legs.

After the flight, he said, "Next time, we're going in a completely new direction. One that you're not comfortable with. You're a good pilot, Terri, and you need to expand your flight skills. You're capable of much more than you think."

Staying in our comfort zones, maintaining our usual patterns, is so easy. I often refer to this as an *inertia problem*. Sometimes, we need a nudge to move us in a new and different direction. We can nudge ourselves or rely on others for a little push. Sometimes we have a choice. Other times . . . well, we have *no* choice.

As we explore new areas and take new risks (big or small), it's so important to have a few people who see what we can be. For example, Paul sees me as a better pilot, and I trust him.

If you don't have these people, (it helps to have different ones for different aspects of your life), find them. Cultivate those relationships, and be that person for others. The world can be a harsh place and make us feel less than we are.

Not feeling bold? Take the courageous step anyway. There's juicy goodness on the other side!

TAKING THE CONTROLS

— What am I most afraid of?
— What can I do despite being afraid?
— How can I get out of my own way?

BRIEFING NOTES

....

....

....

....

....

....

....

....

....

....

....

....

....

....

....

....

....

....

....

....

....

....

Validating My Own Worth:
I Am Enough

A quirky and inspiring picture popped up on my social media feed a few months ago. In the picture was a woman wearing shorts and a Batman mask, sitting casually in a chair, drinking a glass of wine. Her attitude and posture said, *I don't give a fuck* (IDGAF) and screamed of sheer badassery. I wanted to be her. I *want* to be her.

I've spent too much time and energy looking to others for their acceptance to validate my own sense of self-worth. When I am insecure and not feeling like I am enough, I try too hard to make something work without realizing that the situation isn't healthy for me.

Two years of attempting to fit into Sand Hill Angels as an angel investor passed before I realized that it wasn't a good fit for me. I finally opted out after what Bev called "unnecessary suffering." She was right. I should have left sooner.

Other times I appear distant (or needy), making it difficult for others to approach and connect.

On the last night of my first trip to Necker Island, I left the dance party at the main house and wandered around the island looking for something. I didn't know what, but it was my last night, and I wanted it to be great.

A gal from Australia nearly ran me down with a golf cart. I hopped into the cart, and we started chatting. We hadn't spent much time together up until this point. I asked her why we hadn't connected sooner.

She said, "I was intimidated by you and didn't feel comfortable approaching. I wasn't the only one to feel this way."

Yikes!

Apparently, I had been putting off some negative vibes. The truth stunned me, but I realized that in her somewhat drunken state, she'd communicated the most insightful of observations. At the time, I didn't feel as if I belonged, so I put up an invisible shield that made it hard for others to connect with me. In looking for the validation of others, to feel like I belonged, I created a powerful barrier made up of my imposter syndrome and insecurities and missed out on opportunities to connect with some amazing people.

I created my own shitty, circular situation just because I didn't think I was *enough*.

I thought about this the next day as we said our goodbyes. It haunted me on the long trip home. When Bev and I reconnected a year later, we concluded that I had been looking for the wrong thing . . . for others to validate my worth.

No one can do that.

Only I can.

CHAPTER 13

UNEXPECTED OPPORTUNITIES AND SERENDIPITY

Connecting is my superpower, and I love wielding it.

I connect people. I connect ideas. I connect people with ideas.

I spoke on this topic at a women's conference in San Francisco a few years ago. I shared stories on how I got from point A to point F (or point X), including the story about how a very short helicopter ride at an airshow when I was eight led to my playing tennis on Necker Island with Richard Branson. I connected the following points in time:

A. After a short flight at the Hayward Airport in 1978, I said to myself (and no one else), "I want to fly one of these things one day."

B. I finally shared the dream with my husband when I was thirty-two, and he gave me a discovery flight for my thirty-eighth birthday.

C. While training for my private helicopter rating, I met a guy named Stu, who was also learning to fly helicopters. We became friends.

D. A few years later, I told Stu I needed something new, and he suggested angel investing and introduced me to Sand Hill Angels.

E. While part of that group, a gentleman named Ryan shared the opportunity to go to Necker Island. I grabbed it with both hands.

F. While on the island, I played tennis every day and eventually played with Richard.

It makes sense when I lay it out in a logical path, but there's no way I could have planned that out. To the hundred or so women in the conference room that day, I said, "Sometimes, planning isn't the answer. Sometimes, it's a matter of saying *yes* to one thing, which leads to something else. Ultimately, it leads to something completely and totally unexpected. But, without doing the first thing, you will never get to the fabulous end point."

In midlife, when we see the next half of our lives as open terrain, it can be difficult to see the path. In some cases, what we want may not even exist yet. Or the timing may not be right, or we may not be ready.

That's where courage, curiosity, and serendipity come in. When our hearts and minds are open, we can't help but stumble into goodness.

RIGHT IN HER BACKYARD

Bev had a successful career counseling practice in Connecticut when she and her husband decided to move to their vacation home in Cape Cod, Massachusetts.

Her business relied almost 100% on her solid reputation and referrals, but the town they lived in had suburbanized. They'd grown tired of the long commute to where they *really* wanted to live.

Bev talked herself into a program management role in a large government agency that served the unemployed but quickly realized that she wasn't well suited to work for someone else.

"I don't know what I was thinking," she told me. "I let wanting to live a mile away from the ocean get in the way of what I knew about who I was. I'd been an entrepreneur since I started giving piano lessons at fourteen. When I realized my mistake, I graciously outplaced myself from my new job, felt like a failure, and laid in our hammock for a week, depressed. I'd closed a business I loved that served business professionals and now lived in a place surrounded by water and no corporate headquarters. Then I remembered all the training

I'd done with William Bridges, a well-known author, speaker, and organizational consultant, and decided to work the transition model I'd taught so many others.

"I would drive around and get lost, on purpose, and explore any building in town that was more than two stories high to see if it housed a business. I networked with the heads of local chambers of commerce and nonprofit organizations. I offered my services to an economic development agency. I took a class at the community college. I discovered that there was more going on in this tourist mecca than I thought. Soon, I found local clients and continued to work with former clients by phone. I used my Cape location to attract new clients to come to me!

"To my amazement, my new rural home was within biking distance of the Cape Cod Institute and the Gestalt International Study Center (a world-renowned professional development center), where I was able to access extensive training with thought leaders in organizational development, psychology, and the Gestalt coaching model, which gave me a solid foundation to add executive coaching to my practice and work with dynamic, leading-edge thinkers."

It was all right in her backyard.

ON A MISSION TO GIVE BACK

Carliza's son was six when she took her first big trip away from home.

Her friend Melanie volunteered to go on a ten-day mission to Belize to provide free dental care to the locals and asked Carliza to go.

"I decided to go because I wanted to support Melanie. I was surprised by how much I enjoyed the trip and the work. I came back and told my husband I wanted to make more trips like this. I made a resolution to do a mission every year but wasn't able to go again until last year. Between the demands of my own dental practice and my son, I just couldn't make it work."

Carliza didn't realize that first Belize mission would spark a desire to use her professional expertise to give back to the world. Carliza is a first-generation immigrant. "I came to America with my parents when I was a young child. My parents instilled a great work ethic in me. My mother was a woman dentist, a minority, and had to prove herself. I became a dentist, but I wanted greater life balance."

When Carliza's son went off to college, Melanie invited her to join a mission to the Philippines, Carliza's birth country. The opportunity and timing finally worked for Carliza, so she went.

Carliza is not alone in feeling that everything she has done up until now (years of schooling, work, continuing education, and her commitment to the advancement of the dental industry) has been worth it.

She said, "I feel more valuable. It feels like all of the years of school and work were worth it."

For many midlife women, giving back becomes important, especially in areas of professional expertise and experience.

While she couldn't go on mission trips, Carliza became active in the California Dental Association when her son was in middle school. She was in her early forties at the time. Now that he's in college, she has even more time to find ways to give back and leverage her extensive experience as a dentist. Her next mission is to Uganda. I can't wait to see where she goes next!

TAPPING INTO THE UNEXPECTED

Julie decided at forty that she wanted to challenge herself physically. She started training for half marathons, specifically the Nike Half Marathon. As soon as she successfully completed it, she signed up for another. I asked her how many she'd run. She laughed and said, "I've lost count."

When she was forty-five, she said, "I needed to up the ante. I signed up for a marathon and started training. My dad started running in his fifties and still runs in his seventies, so I have a great running role model.

"The marathon went great. The second one was a challenge, though. I made it halfway through and knew I could suffer through it, but didn't want to or need to. I thought, *a half marathon is respectable. I don't want to hurt myself. I can stop now.* And I did. I thought my dad would think it was funny."

She turned fifty and wanted to challenge herself yet again, so she went to Bali for a yoga retreat. "Going to Southeast Asia was like a marathon for me; it was a bit out of my comfort zone, and the travel was challenging. But I knew it was going to be a spiritual place, so I went with an open heart and mind. While there, the work that I did helped me access places deep inside myself for the first time.

"I am more trusting now. I know I have more to tap into internally than ever before. I no longer look to others to make things better. And my relationship with my husband went to a new level. We've always had a good relationship, but it's even better now. There's no tension or stress. We can let things go. Once I stopped trying to change him and decided to believe that he was always doing the best that he could with what he had at the moment, and he started to do the same, things really changed for the better."

Her kids called her *Deepak Mom* when she got back, which really meant, "Stop coaching me, Mom!"

"I listened to them and backed off. I decided to let them do them."

LIVING LOCALLY IN A FOREIGN LOCALE

If some of my friends from high school hadn't posted pictures of their six-week Paris sojourn on social media, my family would never have known about home exchanges.

Pictures of a trip to France kept popping into my feed long after most people were back to work. Finally, I asked if they'd moved to

Paris. "No," said Richard, "we swapped houses with a family in Paris. We head home next week."

"Tell me more!" I said immediately.

Through a website called HomeExchange, they'd swapped houses with a family there. The idea inspired me, but I took no action until our dog died the following February. We would either get a new dog or find a way to spend a month in Paris.

We ended up in Paris.

It took seven months to find a French family interested in coming to Redwood City, where we live. We live halfway between San Francisco and San Jose, but most people want to be in a city rather than the suburbs. As luck would have it, the family we ended up swapping with had friends in the adjacent cities, San Carlos and Menlo Park.

Serendipity? Yep!

We arrived at their place in France in time to meet them, exchange keys, and help them into a cab as they departed for the airport. We met a U.S. neighbor for lunch that day, a block from where we stayed in the 17th arrondissement in Paris, and I ended up going clubbing with her that night. If I hadn't gone, I would have missed out on having drinks in a birdcage near the Moulin Rouge.

Jet lag persists for a week, so what's a few more lost hours of sleep?

We managed to explore quite a bit of Paris, shop in the local markets, and cook French food in France with French ingredients. Eat your heart out, Julia Child!

Everyone was remarkably delightful and supportive as I practiced my French (as did the kids). Since we also swapped cars, we drove to Normandy and Champagne. Driving a stick shift in Paris is akin to driving the Grand Prix, especially around the Place de la Concorde, which we dubbed the *circle of death*.

Two summers later, we did two more exchanges. Fourteen days in Paris and three weeks in Provence. What did we get out of these experiences? Expanded perspectives. We got outside of our comfort zones. We experienced the reality of being foreigners figuring out the local way of doing things. And we made some unforgettable memories. All of which made us better people.

How did all of this come about?

Because I saw something that struck my interest, and I asked my friend a question.

Would we have been able to do it in our thirties? Probably not. But in midlife, it seems that *things* matter much less than *experiences*. Things come and go, but memories?

They last a lifetime.

TAKING THE CONTROLS

— What opportunity can I say *yes* to?
— Where does serendipity show up in my life?
— What is my superpower?

BRIEFING NOTES

WHEN ONE DOOR CLOSES . . .

I was thirty-five when I was laid off for the second time from a bio-tech company. I had been laid off twice in three years and decided it was time to take control of my own destiny.

Bev often says that when people lose their jobs, it's an invitation to rethink, to grow, and to develop. I wholeheartedly agree. Getting laid off can be devastating, even when you didn't want to be at that job, but great things may come of it.

The first time I was laid off, I hated the company I was working for and actually thanked the CIO for laying me off and providing a severance package. I still remember the stunned look on his face. Of course, I still felt like shit. Not everyone got laid off, and I wondered why I wasn't good enough to keep around.

Same thing happened the second time. The company was tanking, and I knew it wasn't a good place for me . . . yet I once again felt as if something were wrong with me. Why didn't they want to keep *me*?

After the second layoff in June 2005, I took my severance package, said thank you and goodbye, and started my consulting company, Solutions2Projects, LLC. I spent that summer getting into great shape swimming masters at my local pool two to three times a week. I spent time with my kids as we moved them to a daycare closer to our house. By October, I had my first client. It was time for me to, as Bev said, "Rethink it, grow, and develop."

In 2019, I celebrated fourteen years of being in business. Business was great for many years. I had multiple clients and projects running at the same time. I brought on consultants as subcontractors to meet the demand. I evolved the business as technology and regulations changed and to meet my clients' demands and needs.

But, over the past two years, things have changed. The work I used to do has pretty much disappeared, as if the faucet has slowly turned off and is now at a trickle.

What's a girl to do?

Change with the times, and create new opportunities!

A friend encouraged me to get into expert witness work, so I continue to lay the groundwork, build my network, and increase my credibility. I've shifted my focus into a few new areas and have changed my messaging around the work. I've created a new company, Class Bravo Ventures, for new services in the digital health space, and am combining my previous consulting experience with newly gained investing knowledge to create a whole new service offering.

Here's the thing. The work that dried up? It was work I didn't want to be doing anyway. But I couldn't let go of it because it had been so good to me financially. Plus, it was really easy to do.

I'd been on autopilot, and the universe decided to give me a kick in the ass to make me make the change (kind of like when I was laid off the second time). I finally got the message. I was freaking out as I reworked my LinkedIn profile and website. Once I hit the delete button and created the language for the new service offering, however, I felt freedom and excitement as I let go of the drag.

For a lot of us, we need something to end before we can move on to the next big and amazing thing. It can be hard to let go. It's easier to remain in a comfy spot even when something isn't really that good or is no longer serving us.

When a door hits us on the ass on our way out, there's often something exciting waiting for us on the other side.

CHAPTER 14
MAINTENANCE
AND SELF-CARE

The things that replenish my energy and my soul often surprise me. For the last few years, I've been mentoring a woman back east. We've never met in person, but we get on a call every three to six weeks to discuss what's top of mind for her. I've supported her through job changes and work challenges, but we always make time for the human conversations. We talk about tennis, our families, and our travels. And, sometimes, books.

The other day my energy was a little low when we got on our scheduled call. I mentally set aside whatever I was dealing with and made myself present for her. She talked about having a great trip to Cuba with her husband. We talked about the passing of her aunt and how the demands of others can grind us down. Eventually, the conversation switched to books before we ended the call.

The call left me feeling *good*. Supporting and encouraging her elevated my mood. I looked back and saw a pattern in the history of our calls. After every single one of my calls with her, I felt reenergized.

After the call, I created a list of what refuels me so that when I feel depleted, I have a few options. (Then I lost the list. Go figure!)

Self-care takes many forms, including exercise, healthier eating habits, massages, eliminating toxic people, getting out into nature, sleep, taking a break, and finding things to feed your soul.

For example, many of us need to redefine why we exercise as we get older. For most of us, it's less about proving anything to anyone else and more about making sure we're strong and healthy.

Jackie Pilossoph says in her article, "Be Kind to the Perimenopausal Women in Your Life"[22] that "perimenopausal women need self-care more than ever because of hormonal changes and inconsistent symptoms that are ultimately causing stress fatigue."

Cheri Stefanelli, a community health educator, personal trainer, and fitness/yoga instructor, says in the same article, "Everything is unpredictable and inconsistent, and you can't pinpoint it. It can mess with your head and whatever you have known to be normal."

Um, yeah.

Every day I wonder if this is a new normal or a temporary side effect of perimenopause.

SELF-CARE IS NON-NEGOTIABLE

For Cathy, certain things are non-negotiable, like her daily workout. She enjoys the endorphins, and the workout helps with her anxiety and stress, especially since she reached menopause.

"I used to be a busy executive and considered myself a badass. I thought I was tough and could power through, and I didn't want to be seen as weak. With each new responsibility I took on, there was less and less time for self-care, and I suffered as a result," she said as we enjoyed a glass of wine over lunch, something she never would have done before.

"I try to get out into my garden on the weekends to play in the dirt. As I've expanded my professional network, I've met more women and developed new friendships, especially with younger women. I now make time for friends and socialization. I feel much more well balanced."

These may seem simple, but all make her mind and body healthier. Her old way of *powering through* wouldn't have been sustainable with menopause and her professional responsibilities, nor would it best position her for later in life.

PRACTICAL SELF-CARE

Julie is forty-seven, has two kids, holds a demanding job at a prominent tech company, and has always made staying physically healthy a priority. It shows. She always looks great.

"It used to be all about marathons and kickboxing, but now it's all about whatever fits into my family and work schedule. I slip out of the office between meetings and walk when I am at work. Once a week, I step it up and get in a run. And my husband and I get some time to chat as we walk during our son's soccer practices. I try to eat healthy with a focus on moderation and balance."

In midlife, she's much more in tune with her body than ever before. She's added weights into her weekly program because it's good for her bones.

"I try to fit in quarterly facials, and I take a bath with a good book as often as I can," she said. "I read every night and love a good book, whether it's fiction, non-fiction, or a short story or two."

Once her children are out of the house, she knows there will be more time for herself. Until then, she's doing what she can to stay healthy and in shape in a way that is better suited for her current life.

SELF-CARE IDEAS

Women often struggle with self-care because we've spent our lives taking care of others. Then we find, in midlife, we often don't know how to care for ourselves. Here are a few ideas that might not show up on your typical list.

1. Nature

Get out into nature. This can be gardening, a hike in the woods, a stroll along the beach, or a multi-day camping trip in the wild. If you live in a city or don't have access to a garden, find a way to step out and look at the trees, listen to the birds, maybe take your shoes off and walk barefoot in the grass or sand. Reconnect with nature on a spiritual and physical level. Hug a tree.

It's the ultimate in self-care.

Julia Cameron, in her book *It's Never Too Late to Begin Again*, says, "When we connect with nature, we forge further connections to those around us, to our higher self, to our past, and our future. Our world expands."

Nature improves mental and physical health. This includes reducing stress and inflammation, improving short-term memory, eliminating fatigue, reducing depression and anxiety, lowering blood pressure, boosting your immune system, and improving your ability to focus. Given that most of these are symptoms of perimenopause, it seems that we should take a break and go play outside.

Gardening is a metaphor for midlife. We're eliminating weeds, trimming back the things (and people) that may be getting out of control, and planting something new.

2. Shake Up Your Use of Social Media

With social media, it seems like one moment you feel like you're connected to the world, and the next you wonder how you got so lost.

My son pointed out recently that we tend to only put our *best* on social media. I couldn't disagree with him because, really, who wants to read depressing stuff when you're trying to escape from your own life? Confession: I mostly post the good stuff and the curated pictures taken from the best possible angle.

Yet again, the comparison game is self-torture and self-sabotage.

If we assume that social media provides the full picture, we'll never be happy or satisfied. I wonder how the hell some people stay so thin or afford yet another vacation. I have to tell myself, "Stop. Back up the truck."

Then I find a different perspective.

I look at the travel pictures, and I am happy that they had an adventure. Their joy does not detract from mine. I can live vicariously (in a positive way) through their pictures and their happiness.

You've got pictures of Paris to share? Share on! I will reminisce about my great times in France and get inspired to make croissants or *boeuf bourguignon*. I might even put on some Edith Piaf or practice some French on Duolingo.

You're sailing in the British Virgin Islands?

My heart may hurt for a moment as I remember the amazing feeling on Necker Island, but I won't fight the feeling. I'll let it sit, then remember how I was inspired to do bigger things in the world because I went. I'll feel gratitude for even having had the opportunity.

Some days are easier than others. I'm sure that people have seen my pictures and wondered how I hit the jackpot. I live a rich, adventurous, joyous, and eventful life!

If we think about what we post, how we curate it, and imagine others doing the same, it's much easier to find perspective. If it gets to be too much, walk away from it. Or take a short break, and detox from the crack that is social media. Sometimes, we are better off without it.

3. Run Away with the Circus

There are some days that I want to run away to the circus, preferably the *Night Circus*, which is one of my all-time favorite books. This isn't much of a stretch given that I come from European circus people on my mom's side, and I love the flying trapeze.

But why? you might be asking.

My life often feels like a three-ring circus. Despite my husband staying home, I, like most women, carry a lot of the mental and emotional load. Some days it's too much. Inevitably, I reach a max point and have no idea what to do. I just want to run away for a little bit.

One particular night, my son, who had been very difficult and was criticizing me and my efforts and blaming me for things I hadn't even done, became exuberant with his appreciation toward his father. At that point, I hit my limit. My feelings were hurt.

I calmly walked to my room (with a glass of wine), closed the door, climbed into bed, closed my eyes, and mentally ran away to the circus. I imagined the cute outfits and cotton candy and daring feats of wonder.

And magic. *Lots* of magic.

At times like this, I find it best to take a break. Read a book. Escape into another world. Watch a movie like *A Wrinkle in Time* (written by and for women) or *Chocolat*. Step into someone else's imagination. Close your eyes, and create your own mental fantasy to give yourself a break from reality.

That's exactly what I did that night.

And it worked.

4. Add a Little Sparkle

A little extra sparkle maintains my sanity and protects those around me.

Sometimes, it's just a pedicure with an added layer of gold glitter. Sometimes, I add some bubbly (the French kind) along with some no-BS time with friends. It's amazing how quickly I can swing from feeling like it's all under control one day, to being completely whackadoodle the next, then to regaining some balance that very evening.

On those days, I try to treat myself with much-deserved love and kindness and take a few extra breaths.

Sometimes, I even put on a tiara. There's always an extra one in my glovebox. And I recently discovered that Tiara Tank Top Tuesday is a thing. I triple dog dare you!

5. Be Your Own Valentine

I believe in sharing the love every day in February.

This is why I send out Valentines instead of holiday cards. And why I cut out construction paper hearts for my husband and kids each and every day in February. I write something I love about them and tape the hearts to their bedroom doors. It's kind of a daily grat-itude to my family.

What about showing myself some love?

Well, there's been a little bit of extra vitamin P (for pleasure) with the new toys I bought, all in the name of research for chapter sixteen. *Nudge, nudge; wink, wink.* I've also been setting better boundaries, asking for help, and eliminating toxic people.

What can you do?

Want fresh-cut flowers in your house? Grab a pretty vase, and cut some from your garden, or buy a small bouquet at your local market. I like putting them on my nightstand or in the bathroom.

Write yourself some love notes on construction paper hearts, and put them somewhere only you can see.

Use the fancy lotion or bath oil you've been saving for a special occasion.

Dig out an old gift certificate, and spend it on yourself. We all have those sitting around in a drawer or the bottom of our purses.

Savor a moment with a cup of your favorite coffee or tea in a beautiful mug or teacup. Alone. Or with a good friend.

Whatever you choose, make sure it is a tribute of love and good-ness to yourself.

6. Receive Something Because it Feels so Good

As an over-giver, I have a terrible time receiving. One morning recently, I practiced receiving, and I have to say . . . it felt really good.

Twice.

The previous Sunday night, I ordered a Lioness vibrator from Liz Klinger, the founder of Lioness.io. I was doing research on sex in midlife in the twenty-first century, and the Lioness is a con-nected vibrator that gives you data about your orgasms. So, not your mother's vibrator!

Liz volunteered to bring me my order the day after I ordered it, and initially, I declined. I didn't want to trouble her, which meant I didn't think I was worth her time. She insisted, and I relented. She drove over an hour and stayed to discuss sex and technology and what they are trying to do with Lioness.

Impressive stuff.

So, how did I practice receiving? I will leave that up to your imagination, but I will say that she brought me the gift that keeps on giving, and I have the data to prove it!

7. Know When to Stop

Paige struggled to recover from some health issues while experiencing chronic fatigue. Her body was sending her a very loud and clear message that something had to change.

"I was used to having boundless energy and grew frustrated with my body. I couldn't understand why I couldn't do all that I had done before. This made me depressed."

She sought help for her depression, decided to listen to her body, and began to make some changes. She no longer powers through days like she used to. She stops when she gets tired. She schedules weekly massages and manicures to relieve stress and pamper herself. She told me, "If I ignore the fatigue and just keep going, I pay a high price with my body and my health. I am more in tune with my body and am able to listen to it better. I am better off overall."

Lately, I've been giving myself permission to not put in sixteen-hour days and simply relax in the evening with my husband, my kids, or just my dog and a book. Letting go of the need to check one more thing off the list or be *productive* all the time feels good. Permission to stop and take breaks—or sit and watch YouTube videos of *The Voice*, *PokerStars*, or *Lip Sync Battle*—is OK. And it's OK to sit in the sun and listen to the chickens or watch my cat chase squirrels (catch them and eat their feet . . . yuck!).

Our bodies are working overtime handling hormonal changes,

brain changes, and transitions. Pushing through, trying to get one more thing done, is going to make it even harder. We end up depleted after digging deep, over and over, for more energy.

If we don't stop ourselves, eventually, our bodies will.

TAKING THE CONTROLS

— What refuels me?
— What can I do to take better care of myself?
— How can I make self-care a priority?

BRIEFING NOTES

On Botox

Our society celebrates youth and hasn't learned to value women as we age.

A few years ago, a friend of mine commented on the divot in my forehead between my eyebrows and suggested that I get Botox. I was around forty-five, and it hadn't occurred to me to do anything artificial. In my thirties, I swore I would never do anything like Botox or plastic surgery, delusionally stating that we should embrace our bodies and faces as we age.

Being from Northern California, I thought we were immune to the vanities of L.A. but quickly realized I was wrong. We are in Silicon Valley, after all. My friend introduced me to her plastic surgeon, and it wasn't long before I was in his office having toxins painfully injected into my forehead.

I was surprisingly pleased with the results and can clearly see the difference in pictures. I play a game inside my head where I assess whether a photo was taken before or after Botox. Turns out, it wasn't the divot that was the problem, but the general forehead wrinkles.

My daughter called them *stripes* when she saw them on my husband's forehead. He isn't bothered by his stripes or the silver in his hair or graying beard. Why should he be? Not only does he look better than ever, but men are allowed to age. Women are expected to prevent the slip into *old hag*.

Various movements for women to *embrace the gray* are popping up. They're meant to encourage more women not to dye their hair and to celebrate their stripes. To embrace the naturally occurring stretch marks that come with growth, weight gain, and childbirth. A quick Google search on the campaigns for women to accept their stretch marks revealed a plethora of advertisements for stretch mark disappearance products.

The title of one of the so-called articles was "The Negative Impact of Stretch Marks on Women's Body Image" and referenced a study of women surveyed. Turns out that the company that funded the study was one of the magic cream companies.

Our enemy is not age, but the media and product companies creating—or capitalizing on—the insecurities of aging women. The pressure to always be *more* of something, *less* of something else, and to walk the tightrope of acceptable behavior, is ridiculous. I, for one, would like to see more campaigns that stop putting women in tidy, little boxes.

This reminds me of something I heard on a podcast. I love the Commonwealth Club's *Week to Week Political Roundtable*. One episode, they discussed Kamala Harris and her campaign playbook, qualifications, and demeanor.

At one point, one of the male panelists commented on how Kamala needed to try to appear more likable and warm to be effective. Didn't we learn anything from how Hillary Clinton was treated on the campaign trail in 2016? No one is suggesting that Bernie or Biden needs to be more likable.

The sole female panelist, Melissa Caen, called them out for even suggesting it, and they backtracked on their comments. This isn't the end of the national conversation on the likability of female candidates; others are encountering the same shit. It's never about their competence and experience. It's always about a bar that keeps moving, keeping us off-balance and constantly reminding us that we don't belong.

It's time we've had enough.

**As I continue to fight for women, I will continue to get my quarterly poison injection so that I don't look as mad or tired!

CHAPTER 15

FLIGHT CREW: IMPORTANCE OF SUPPORT AND FRIENDSHIP

"I feel so emotionally raw as we get closer to Adam's high school graduation day," I said to my friend, Maggie, as we walked onto the tennis court. "Is it easier for you since Heather is your second child graduating and heading off to college after Melanie?"

Maggie and I have known each other for years but rarely see each other outside scheduled tennis matches. She responded, "You'd think so, but this time it's actually harder. Melanie was much quieter and kept to herself, but Heather interacts with both of her younger brothers. Her absence will be much more noticeable when she leaves this fall."

I went on to lose a great match but couldn't get this conversation out of my mind. I reached out to Maggie and a few other moms who were sending their firstborn kids off to college and arranged for a night of champagne, snacks, and conversation.

And thus, a new crew was born.

People come and go in our lives. We get busy with all of the demands on our time and attention from our significant others, children, aging parents, and jobs or businesses, and it's easy to stop making time for friendships and those who enrich our lives and replenish our souls. Friendship requires time—time we often choose to spend in support of others and not ourselves.

In midlife, this needs to be a priority. It's good for our health, our sanity, and our mental acuity.

But not all friendships are the same. Friendships are like wine. Some age well, and some turn into vinegar. Most of us change and grow over time, but some friends don't want to adjust or change.

Some become bitter and are better left behind. Some opt out on their own.

As we move through midlife, not everyone is going to be coming along for the ride. Like the game of Life, people get in and out of our car. We need to focus on those who support our growth and evolution. Change can be uncomfortable, painful, exciting, overwhelming, and scary, but is always necessary.

We need deep and supportive friendships later in life. If we don't assess our friendship situation now, we're going to run out of time.

Full-bodied, complex, textured wine takes time. You can't rush it. There are no shortcuts. Trusting, reliable, and true friendships need time too.

FRIENDSHIP

"Friends are like the Swiss Army knife of relationships. They do everything: boosting your health, lengthening your life, preserving your memory, helping your career, gentling the aging process," says Rebecca Adams, a sociologist and gerontologist from the University of North Carolina at Greensboro in the book, *Life Reimagined.*

Maintaining friendships and making friends gets more difficult as we get busy, especially if we have spouses, children, and/or demanding careers. Not only are we battling friendship conflicts, but due to hectic lives, we often prioritize our family first.

Rebecca goes on to say in a separate article, "It becomes tougher to meet the three conditions that sociologists since the 1950s have considered crucial in making close friends: proximity; repeated, unplanned interactions; and a setting that encourages people to let their guard down and confide in each other."[23]

Single women (assuming without kids or with kids who are out of the house) do a better job with building and maintaining friendships. If a woman doesn't have a significant other or children, these friends become surrogate families.

Eric Klinenberg, author of *Going Solo: The Extraordinary Rise and Surprising Appeal of Living Alone*, says, "Those who live alone have fewer constraints on their time and fewer responsibilities to others, which means they can be open to new experiences, and they can throw themselves into intense personal situations." For these women, he sees friendships building around life stages and not just age.

For Gen Xers, regardless of marital or parental status, this makes a lot of sense. We aren't all moving collectively through the same life stages as generations before us. We connect with women of all ages because of shared interests and don't see age as a barrier.

This also means taking a look at the people in our lives and making choices about who should be in it. I saw a clip on social media where Trent Shelton talked about adding to your life by subtracting from it.

He went on to say:

- Don't confuse the length of a relationship with the strength of the relationship.
- Don't let your loyalty be your slavery. Be loyal to yourself first.

As we go through midlife and explore who we are, being intentional in seeking out new people is a necessity. It's also a byproduct of exploration and experimentation.

In Silicon Valley, I live in a bubble, but it's a pretty diverse bubble. At the same time, I catch myself taking the easy path and gravitating toward people who are like me. I'm sure it's because it feels good and feels familiar.

Meeting people who aren't like us is good for our brains. "When people are exposed to a more diverse group of people, their brains are forced to process complex and unexpected information. The more people do this, the better they become at producing complex and unexpected information themselves."[24]

And who knows where this all might take us in our midlife journey?

The bottom line is that if we want to avoid or reduce significant health risks, decrease loneliness, and increase overall life satisfaction, we must invite new people into our lives, let go of others, and invest in the right friendships during midlife.

FAMILY

Speaking of family, both extended and immediate, we need to raise the bar beyond blood or marriage.

This has been the toughest part for me as my extended family has drifted apart. As a result, I've had to reconstruct who I am and how I see family.

At a time when we're redefining who we are, what we want, and where we want to go, family relationships need to evolve with us. If they don't, that's where we might need to make some tough decisions.

I know I have.

It's not just about friends and family. There are other people that we can bring into our lives to provide us with the support we need to thrive in midlife. We can hire coaches, therapists, dietitians, healthcare providers, housekeepers, people to wait in line for us, and more to help us thrive, fill in the gaps, and contribute to our richest possible lives. We can surround ourselves with people who support and love us. We deserve it.

We can let go of people who aren't serving us.

We can ask for help.

We don't have to go it alone.

FRIENDS ARE VITAL TO YOUR HEALTH

Headlines and articles on a new public health issue keep cropping up everywhere: *Americans over the age of forty-five are lonely.*

Lisa Marsh Ryerson of the AARP Foundation says, "Social

isolation and loneliness have been found to have health risks equivalent to those of obesity or smoking fifteen cigarettes per day."[25]

Scientific research has shown that loneliness raises blood pressure, dumps stress hormones in your bloodstream, and leads to tissue damage and all manner of disease over time. In other words, "Loneliness makes healthy people sick . . . and makes sick people die faster."[26]

Yikes! That's brutal.

All is not lost. Research has shown that having deep, meaningful friendships can decrease loneliness, which leads to higher quality of life and decreased health issues. It can even delay the onset of dementia, as reported by Barbara Bradley Hagerty in *Life Reimagined*. Friends are good for your health. In a TedWomen chat from February 2015 with Lily Tomlin, Jane Fonda said, "I have my women friends; therefore, I am. They make me stronger. They make me brave."

For Jane Fonda, her friends help to define her and give her strength. This is true for all of us women. We need friends.

What we may not truly realize is that deep and true friendships can save our lives.

NURTURING FRIENDSHIPS

If you're struggling with making new friends or keeping old friends, you are not alone.

I see a new headline or article every other day on this very topic. These same articles encourage us to make a concerted effort to make new friends with common interests and invest in friendships, both new and old. Add it to the long list of things for us to do to *improve our lives* and *achieve happiness and bliss*.

I know a lot of people, and I have a lot of friends. Yet, when I experience a crisis, I mentally go through my friend Rolodex and find excuses not to reach out to them. It's the middle of their workday. They're in the middle of making dinner or helping kids with homework. They might be at Orangetheory or out for a run. Or, I think, *She has enough of her own problems; how could I possibly burden her with mine?*

The other day, while trying to decide whether to move forward with a publisher, I reached out to a new friend, Amy, who lives in Texas. I wanted to talk it out with someone. I didn't look at the clock or give myself time to think of excuses. I just picked up the phone and called.

The first thing she said was, "I am so honored and flattered that you decided to ask for my help."

Talk about positive reinforcement.

Another friend and I recently spoke about how we wanted to make a habit of communicating on a regular basis. We've both learned it's hard to establish new habits and trust we are valuable enough to the other person to warrant the extra effort.

Jane Fonda brilliantly said, "I see women friends as a renewable source of power."

I totally agree with her.

Renewable or not, for this power to be available to us, we need to choose to put some of our own energy into our friendships. Then this amazing power source is available when we need it.

Dunbar's Number

Robin Dunbar was a British anthropologist who conducted research on primates. After finding a correlation between brain size and social groups, he extrapolated that data to humans and created what is known as Dunbar's number.

Dunbar's number is, essentially, a measure of the number of stable social relationships we can handle. To put it in a different view, consider Dunbar's number to be the number of people you wouldn't feel embarrassed about joining for an uninvited drink if you bumped into them.

Eventually, he came up with the number 150. In general, we can support 150 stable social relationships with other people (some researchers dispute this number).

If you search this out, you'll see the Dunbar number represented as a series of circles. The first circle (the inner circle), is five. The following circles are fifty and then 150 (the next layers are 500 and 1500, but we'll stop at 150).

The circles are dynamic. People can move in and out of our circles at any given time. My husband and kids are in my inner circle. Jacqueline is a fairly permanent fixture now, with the fifth spot rotating based on my friends' availability.

My next circle of fifty continues to shift. It's hard to keep up with. To make this easier, I created a list of people I value and want to maintain or build relationships with. Seems a bit obsessive to me, but it turns out the experts recommend doing this; it helps us keep the practice of building and maintaining friendships a priority in our lives.

We don't need research studies to tell us that trusted and deep friendships don't happen by accident. They require our love and attention.

SITUATIONAL FRIENDS

Research taught me the phrase *situational friend*. While the term was new to me, the experience of a situational friendship was not.

How often have you been friends with the mom of one of your kids' friends, or a coworker, or someone you took a class with, only to have the friendship dissolve and disappear? I wish I'd known this term sooner because I've been confusing true friendship with the surface-level friendship of situational friends.

The process of re-indexing past and present friendships in my brain as either *true* or *situational* has me feeling lighter. I've looked back with gratitude on what I thought were failed friendships when they were simply situational. Basically, I'm pulling a Marie Kondo and saying *thank you*, and letting them go.

It's so liberating!

Knowing this, I can better appreciate the time I have with my situational friends, enjoy the relationship, and move on.

DRIFTING APART

When high school ended, I kept in contact with two people from my graduating class: my husband and my twin sister.

In college, Vivian, whom I met during my freshman year of college, and I were friends until she remarried, had a baby, and moved to Tennessee in her late thirties, never to be heard from again.

Beth lives three hours away from me, and we write each other letters (yes, actual snail mail) every month or so. We see each other every year when we meet up in the wine country.

Bonnie and I maintain our friendship of twenty-seven years via text and meeting up twice a year in person. If the shit hit the fan, we would be there for each other in an instant, regardless of geography.

Jayne and I were pregnant at the same time, and she became like a sister to me. She lives back east, and we see each other every few years and talk every few months.

Why did some friendships endure while others drifted away?

Life gets in the way. Other activities and people take priority. We have less *free* time and tend to spend time with people physically closest to us. Drifting apart is natural.

We also change as we age. Sometimes, friendships don't. Sometimes we have different needs and values over time. When those get out of alignment, friendships struggle to endure.

Social media has brought us back to people we long haven't seen or spoken to in a whole new way—sometimes after decades. My high school organized a reunion about the same time that Facebook was starting to get popular with our age group. My husband and I both reconnected with a lot of people in a fun, entertaining way. For a while. According to Barbara Bradley Hagerty, it's natural for "mid-life people to gravitate toward those who knew them in their purest form, from when they were children."

With a few exceptions, my husband and I have let go of a lot of the same people. Many conversations felt inauthentic or superficial, and our interests and values weren't aligned anymore. Some folks never really grew up. We didn't have much in common besides our diminished Trojan pride, which wasn't enough to maintain the connection.

If we already struggle to find time for the most important people in our lives, drifting away from those who aren't the most important seems to be the path of least resistance. It's something that we can accept and move on from.

Frankly, sometimes maintaining certain friendships is just not worth the time and energy.

LEARNING TO TRUST

When Serena decided to start her company, she didn't share much about what she was doing.

"I didn't want to tell anyone in my typical circles. I was afraid of the criticism and wanted to be the one to decide how my business should unfold . . . without judgment."

She didn't consider that folks in her circles might be helpful and supportive, and also didn't really share much with her husband either. "I got to the point where I didn't think I could keep up my side of the financial bargain, and I felt as if I had to tell him," she said. "I didn't think it was fair to him or my family to continue to keep the business to myself.

"I was at a critical point. I was either going to step up my efforts and really build my dream or call it all off. I laid it out for him. He surprised me by being quite helpful in helping me create a path forward. I'd completely forgotten about how valuable his economics background could be. And he isn't afraid of money and was able to provide a perspective I couldn't have on my own."

He has been incredibly helpful ever since and is now a supportive and invaluable resource for her. This gave her the courage to reach out to some other friends and share what she is working on. They, too, surprised her and have all offered to help.

"This is exactly the opposite of what I expected. I have friends in different time zones around the world, so when I wake up at 3:00 a.m. and can't get back to sleep, I get on WhatsApp, share the issue, get some help, and then get back to sleep. It's brilliant!"

Every once in a while, she looks back, mystified by her earlier unwillingness to tell others about what she was doing. "I know I won't make the same mistake again," she said.

She joined a professional group with a leading business coach and loves the support from the women there.

"I appreciate the communal wisdom and how supportive everyone is in helping each other move forward with their respective businesses. I'm a lot more comfortable asking for help. With others, I know I can move faster. I also recognized that when I am on my own too much, I get way too wrapped up in my head. That's when the negativity surfaces."

When she consults with her available resources, she snaps out of the negative mindset much more quickly.

And for this, she is incredibly grateful, and much happier.

SOMETIMES, YOU HAVE TO GO IT ALONE

Serena isn't the only one who avoided telling others around her what she was going to do before she did it.

Charlotte and her husband planned to move to another country to live out their retirement. "This was a huge move for us, and it was going to seriously impact members of my family," she said. "Despite knowing that my family would resist, this was something I had to do, and I didn't want to be dissuaded. I'd always made decisions based on what others needed. This time I wanted it to be about what I needed."

If she didn't make this move, she was never going to find *her* time. It was now or never.

She and her husband bought their dream retirement house without consulting friends or family. "We came back and told my family once it was done, when it couldn't be reversed. This helped me hold my ground and not do what made my family happy and comfortable," she said. "I have no regrets."

KEEP 'EM IN THE LOOP

As we go on our personal midlife journeys, it's important to keep those who are important to us in the loop.

This doesn't mean we have to consult them or look for feedback (unless we really want it). It's to keep our loved ones clued in.

This can be significant others, children, parents, siblings, and good friends. They may not be ready to hear it or experience it themselves. They may be scared of the changes. But we can help them with their journeys by keeping them informed about ours.

One word of caution: don't let their journeys hold you back.

In my early forties, when I had no idea what was going on with my midlife journey, I don't think I did a great job of sharing with my husband, largely because I was completely in the dark. When I did share something with him, I totally screwed it up. I had no idea what was going on. Now, I include him to help him feel less threatened.

Through an honest conversation, he admitted he'd been harboring resentment toward me. I told him, "My success, my journey, my existence, these don't detract from yours. You be you."

Our relationship shifted. Like gears, we no longer grind

uncomfortably. It used to feel like he tolerated all of my activities, but lately I've felt more supported, like we're partners.

It's a nice feeling.

BUILD YOUR CREW

Last summer, I attended an angel investor summit in Napa, California, and booked a hotel room for myself. I love this conference and was looking forward to seeing folks and playing poker. I had been the only woman at the poker table the year before.

A month before the event, I met with Shannon, one of my new investor gal pals. When she found out I was going to the summit and had booked a room, she said, "That's great. Want to share a room?"

I was a bit taken aback as we had just met but said *yes*. This turned out to be a great decision (despite initial misgivings about not knowing her well and having to share a bathroom). It's a bro-heavy event, and it was nice to have a female to hang out with.

On the last night, two other women I met at the conference stayed in our room for a full-on slumber party. I hadn't done that kind of thing in years—if not decades—and it was a great way to get to know these women better. One of the women, Jenna, even lives around the corner from me. I refer to them as my investor gal pals. We share deals, go to events, and learn from each other.

They are one of my crews.

We all have multiple crews—groups of friends we pull together to support us and so we can support them. Of course, no individual can provide everything we need, which is why we should all have multiple crews. People come into our lives for a reason. It's up to each of us to figure out why and for how long. Or just enjoy the ride! We need crews we can turn to in a crisis, for a drink, to vent, to share good news, to celebrate, to exercise, and to support our business or financial endeavors.

If we haven't been great about this up until this point, midlife is the time to intentionally build your crews. Each person can provide something different. The first step is to recognize what needs you have. The next step is to fill in the gaps.

Exploration and experimentation are helpful here!

While researching, I found an article that highlighted a meet-up for women over the age of fifty in Los Angeles. The meet-up leader put together diverse activities and had (at last count) over 800 members. They went to art galleries, restaurants, film screenings, and more. It can be as easy as finding a crew like this!

In building your crew, don't be afraid to hire help if you can afford it (there are now some reasonably priced online options). You might hire executive coaches, life coaches, therapists, personal trainers, etc. The most important thing is to surround yourself with positive, honest people. Change is hard. Let's find our cheerleaders and support crews and do what we can do to support other women.

We need all the help we can get.

TAKING THE CONTROLS

— Who is in my inner circle of five friends?
— Who is in my next circle of fifty friends?
— Am I doing enough to cultivate these relationships?
— Do I have any friend gaps?

BRIEFING NOTES

MY MOM USED TO BE
MY BEST FRIEND

While growing up, I shared a close connection with my mom.

We had a two-year stint where we weren't as close that started the summer before my freshman year of high school and continued until I was about sixteen. I clearly remember the day the tension broke. We were in a big yelling match, and she chased me up the stairs. She caught up with me, yanked me around, and slapped me across the face. I slapped her right back.

We both looked at each other, stunned.

This was nowhere near normal for us. Then we both started laughing and collapsed onto the stairwell. After that, we were just fine.

While in college, I spent a lot of time with her. We worked for my dad at his accounting firm and had lunch together every day. After college, I continued to see her on an almost-daily basis.

My MBA was almost done when I quit the firm for good. My new husband, new job, and our new life in San Francisco distracted me, but I still talked to her almost every day.

When I became pregnant with my first child, her excitement about becoming a grandma and my nerves about becoming a mother pulled us together again. We compared pregnancy experiences on an almost-daily basis. She was nineteen when she got pregnant with me and my sister; I was thirty.

Once my son was born, my husband's work schedule left me alone on the weekends, so I would stumble into Mom's house, exhausted, and she would say, "I'll take the baby. You go to bed. I'll wake you when he needs to eat."

As she *found herself* (finally!) and made new friends, our relationship changed. To some extent, I became a pass-through to the kids. There was no longer any mother/daughter time. I was busy running a business, raising a family, and trying to keep my head above water. I didn't force any one-on-one time. I also learned that I had to be careful about what I shared with her when I was wobbly because her fearful concerns for me became my fear. The ease between us faded.

When my sister and I had issues, she felt trapped in the middle. Eventually, I lost a confidant to share my pain and confusion with. As the family drama increased, I chose not to be a part of it. I chose not to play the game by the previously set rules. I chose to not simply accept the relationship as it was because she was my mother. While this was incredibly difficult, I realized I needed to create what I wanted with my relationships, to make sure they work for me out of choice and not obligation. I needed (and continue to need) healthier relationships.

Now, we're both working on rebuilding the relationship. I'm hopeful that it can once again be close, safe, loving, supportive, and fulfilling for both of us.

CHAPTER 16

SEX AND RELATIONSHIPS

"Sex is an elaborate cocktail of our identities, our feelings, our desires, and actions," says Shadeen Francis, a relationship therapist based in Philadelphia.[27]

Isn't that the truth!

In our twenties, we have biology on our side. A drive to procreate. Responsibilities, careers, and parenting cause a dip in sex drive in our thirties. In our forties, hormone changes can be a bad thing for your libido. At the same time, freedom from risk of pregnancy (assuming you're postmenopausal) and a greater awareness of your needs and wants can cause an uptick in desire that can jumpstart a previously sleepy and/or unsatisfying sex life.

Feel like a bit of a mixed message?

Well, really, it is.

According to Maxine Barish-Wreden, MD, "Good sex is a quality of life issue. It affects the quality of our relationships and how we feel about ourselves." She encourages individuals in a relationship to talk to their partners about what is going on, because sexual intimacy leads to emotional intimacy.

"Many aspects of sexual interest and libido are in the brain, not just the body. Maintaining sexual interest involves enlisting a strong mind and body connection."[28]

Consider talking to your doctor about what's going on if you think something feels off or has changed. Some things may be normal and treatable, and others not. Sexual health and wellness should be part of our healthcare provider discussions.

"8 Reasons Why Sex Is Better After 50"[29] (this is an article from

2012, so it really targeted the Baby Boomers, not Gen X, but a few of the items still made me chuckle) had a few thoughts on sex that I've summarized here:

- Now the sex act is simply that; it can become another fun activity.
- Many women are on their own . . . and while they may occasionally get lonely, they're looking for a good time as often as they're looking for a long-term relationship.
- By the time we hit menopause, we're beyond the conventional *good girl* mentality and into the *Fuck You Fifties*. It's embracing our personal choices without requiring anyone's approval.
- Given that women become risk-takers with age, it seems only natural to try out new acts, positions, and partners.

Pretty inspirational, if you think about it.

Despite the fact that our culture leads us to believe that older women (are we really *older women* in midlife?) don't want to have sex, if we redefine what *sex* means and have the courage to examine relationships that serve our needs, we have an opportunity for a rockin' good time.

WHAT'S LOVE GOT TO DO WITH IT?

Everything!

Jessa Zimmerman, a sex therapist and couples counselor based in Seattle, and I chatted on my podcast. She is a huge proponent of removing expectations around sex and redefining it to be less goal-oriented and more about connection and pleasure. She wrote a book called *Sex Without Stress,* which I ordered. After twenty-three years of marriage, my husband and I have accumulated some baggage and have been paralyzed by expectations.

More on that later.

Jessa says, "We have the opportunity in midlife to reframe and reshape our definition of feelings, beliefs, expectations, and experiences around sex and intimacy and relationships. This is a big part of being human.

"In midlife, we're finally getting more skillful in balancing the tension between our drive for autonomy and our drive for togetherness. We get clearer with our life experiences, wisdom, and strengths of self to really understand our bottom lines. That, in turn, influences our approach to relationships and sex. As we age, we gain clarity and are more honest with ourselves and those around us.

"It is also during this time that we gain the strength to take risks with our relationships. Sometimes this ends the relationship, and other times, it's the beginning of a better and stronger relationship."

We would all benefit from redefining sex and making it something that isn't goal-oriented.

"Sex is about the physical expression of our drives for intimacy and connection. Redefining that for all ages will give us flexibility. We all benefit from a broader definition and understanding of sex."

For some couples, this means that we need to be more creative as both parties age, regardless of gender and couple composition. If we're able to reframe sex as Jessa sees it, opportunities to experience joy and pleasure are unlimited.

BODY CHANGES

There's no denying that the body changes as we age.

Gravity may keep us firmly rooted to the ground, but it isn't good for some of our body parts! Hormonal changes contribute to these changes, which means we look at ourselves in a new way. Looking in the mirror has been tough for me—but looks aren't everything. I've chosen to focus on strength and endurance rather than outward appearances.

Some days are easier than others.

A small study of women between the ages of forty-five and sixty found that some of these women felt more confident and more comfortable in their own skin as they got older, and this allowed them to feel freer in the bedroom.[30] I aspire to be Katherine, the older woman in *Under the Tuscan Sun* who enjoys eating ice cream, talks about ladybugs, and poses naked for lovers a third her age. Her confidence is gorgeous, even if age has taken its toll on her physical shell.

Numerous studies have shown that women who were more comfortable with their own bodies found it easier to orgasm, did so more often, and generally had better sex overall.

If this isn't motivation to accept my body, I am not sure what is.

Some women experience changes, including vaginal dryness, that make for painful sex. Fortunately, we're seeing progress in solutions for this, including natural lubricants, Keurig-like devices to heat up lubricants, and even some medical devices to stimulate vaginal circulation.

A friend of mine is experiencing a post-divorce relationship with a younger man and is enjoying it quite a bit. He appreciates her and enjoys activities that she enjoys, but she is on an antidepressant that makes it difficult for her to have orgasms. She is having to choose between daily sanity and (possibly) daily orgasms.

This gets us back to reframing sex and pleasure—it isn't all about the orgasm.

Liz Klinger, founder of Lioness.io, said while discussing the Lioness vibrator, "Pleasure is an ongoing practice. Part of practicing is knowing yourself, accepting yourself, and learning how to observe and reflect on the thoughts and feelings you have."

SEXPLORATION

I love the idea of sexual exploration (sexploration?) at a time when we have experience behind us (under our belt?) and curiosity is encouraged.

Midlife is a great time to stop assuming we know everything

about our bodies, in terms of pleasure, and start exploring new things. Think of all the fun possibilities!

With the exception of some high-risk behaviors, sexploration could lead to new pleasure discoveries. Now is the time for us to forget what we know, let go of our assumptions, lower our inhibitions, and approach sex without preconceived notions.

INNER SEX KITTEN

When I feel like punishing myself, I look back at some pictures from my early twenties.

My friend Katy took a picture of me when I was twenty, dressed in a French maid's costume, and I looked amazing in a super-short skirt, thigh-high stockings, and high heels.

Ooh la la!

I had just broken off my engagement to a British guy ten years my senior and was interested in a guy closer to my own age. Katy and I were going to a Halloween party, and I thought that dressing up like a French maid was the path to his heart. I spent $110 (a lot of money for a college student in 1990) to rent this costume.

It didn't work.

Fast forward a year, and my husband and I were dating while he was at Chico State in Northern California, and I was living in the San Francisco Bay Area. I drove three hours to Chico wearing a trench coat—and not much else underneath—and surprised him at his doorstep.

I don't think he ever recovered.

This is who I used to be! Somehow, between career, kids, body changes, and the stresses of life, I lost touch with my inner sex kitten.

I've said it before and will say it over and over again—in midlife, we have the opportunity to revisit who we *were* and bring back to life things we set aside as we progressed. The *sex and conquer* mentality of my youth didn't transition well into *love and marriage*.

Fortunately, it isn't too late, and my inner sex kitten is coming out to play and check out some midlife sexploration.

CHEATING AND DIVORCE

Not surprisingly, adultery seems to be both the cause and consequence of a failing marriage. Nicholas Wolfinger, a University of Utah sociologist, found that people born between 1940 and 1959 report the highest rates of extramarital sex. These are the first generations to come of age during the sexual revolution.[31]

While this was fascinating, I was curious about Gen X. Are we more or less prone to cheat and why? I couldn't find much of anything. Like most things with our generation, there's not much out there.

Reasons for cheating range from needing to have emotional needs met to an increase in hormones (in what Michelle Crosby calls a *going-out-of-business sale*[32]), nature's way of saying that if you want a baby, this is your last chance. Other reasons included revenge, father issues, boredom, and low self-esteem. Another was for an aging woman to show she's still got it.

Surprisingly, Gen Xers are not handling divorce like their parents.

In the article, "Generation X Has the Key to a Happy Divorce,"[33] Katherine Woodward Thomas says, "Thanks in large part to the Gen Xers, who grew up swimming in the sewage of their parents' nasty divorces, we're also in the midst of a radical improvement of how we end our long-term romantic relationships, upleveling the typical ugly and contentious breakup to be less bitter and a more benevolent, forgiving experience.

"Gen Xers went through its all-important, formative years as one of the least parented, least nurtured generations in U.S. history. Yet most of us managed to find our way, and some of us even became stronger, more resilient, and more loving people because of all we'd endured. And many who lived through the annihilation of their childhood homes grew up determined to never subject their own children to a shattering similar to the one they'd suffered."

Ms. Woodward Thomas offers an optimistic take. "Gen Xers are the heroes who are willing to stumble about trying to figure out how to remain a loving family after dissolving a marriage—a whole new take on staying together for the sake of the kids. They're endeavoring a recalibration of family that strives to accommodate the growing needs of all of its members."

My friend Andrea and her ex amicably divorced when their daughter was around three. They made every effort to make sure their daughter felt loved. Eventually, they both remarried. At her wedding, Andrea's ex-husband sat at the head table.

"We made a choice to lovingly co-parent our child, and we work hard to make sure we are supportive of each other in life and in parenting our daughter," Andrea said.

Other friends chose to remain in the same house after separating in order to minimize the impact. The wife moved into the garage and created a space for herself. The girls got their own rooms. They've split days in which they are responsible for the girls and make sure the girls know they are a priority.

SOULMATE-SHMOULMATE

A few years ago, I realized that while my husband is great, he can't give me everything I need and want. With this realization came a raised awareness of what I wanted in my life and what I lacked.

My husband and I are really good logistically. We have solid, shared values. We've put the kids first for many years and are at the point where we can put our relationship on a front burner again. Fortunately, we're both interested in a great, long-term relationship—I appreciate how fortunate I am for this to be the case.

At the same time, I swear he either turns off his *listening ears* when I talk, or intentionally ignores a lot of what I say. Whether I ask him a question, request something from the store, or share an interesting part of my day, he doesn't hear the words I say. It comes across as if there's a device between his ears and his brain that excludes words and/or translates them into something completely different. I've confirmed this with others, so I know I'm not crazy. I don't think he's doing it intentionally.

As such, I've found others to listen and provide support. After almost twenty-three years of marriage, I pick my battles.

Lauren Mazzo talks about the false expectation that one person can meet all of our needs. "Instead of treating your S.O. as your number-one confidant, source of intimacy, best friend, lover, and guidance counselor, you should use friends, hobbies, social groups, therapy, and other things to support yourself."[34]

There's way too much hype about *soulmates* and finding *the one*. I think we were fed a bill of goods.

We can all benefit from creating crews of people and participating in activities that provide us with what we need without looking to one person to provide it all.

Taking the Controls

— Am I getting enough vitamin P (passion, pleasure)?
— Is my inner sex kitten awake and fulfilled?
— Is some sexploration in order?

BRIEFING NOTES

....

....

....

....

....

....

....

....

....

....

....

....

....

....

....

....

....

....

....

....

NOT YOUR MOTHER'S VIBRATOR

I discovered orgasms in second grade during gymnastics—the uneven parallel bars were magical at the age of eight. I'm assuming my mother knew why I was always late to the car, but if not, now she knows!

In high school, I discovered sex and multiple orgasms. I enjoyed it immensely and developed a *sex and conquer* mentality. Why were guys allowed to have all the fun, but if we girls did it, we were called sluts?

Really?

I rejected the double standard then and reject it now.

This worked out fine until I was twenty-six and decided to marry my husband, at which time there became a conflict between *sex and conquer* and *love and marriage*. I'd developed a false belief that I could be *in love* and be a *good girl* or be a *bad girl* and love sex.

Not only is this ridiculous, but I can use midlife as the time to explore and discover new things about sex while having a lot of fun! So, under the guise of research, I decided to check out the Lioness vibrator.

I have a plethora of connected devices that capture all sorts of data. A watch that will let me know if I am in atrial fibrillation. A scale that tracks my weight and shows the weather. A meditation device that tells me about my experience.

So why not a connected vibrator?

After Liz brought me the Lioness, I stashed the bag in my room, wondering when I would be brave enough to give it a try.

During my conversation with her, she said, "I created the Lioness for women to use to explore their bodies and their pleasure."

Midlife is the perfect time for us women to throw away all previous expectations and assumptions and discover what makes us feel good. You may have already discovered what works and what doesn't work for you, or you might have found the most expeditious route to satisfaction, whether with a partner or on your own.

In the book, *On Being 40ish,* Jill Kargman, author and actress, contributed an essay which says, "We become balsamic reductions as we age—our very best parts distilled and clarified."

I am pretty sure she wasn't talking about sex.

What if we took on the mindset of a beginner and let go of what we assumed *worked* and tried something new?

What if we took the time to accept our bodies for what they are, accept that things have changed, and used the time to explore and rediscover our inner sex kittens?

In doing the research on sex, I realized that my inner sex kitten was waking up and screaming to get out of the cage I'd put her in. I knew I had to start with *me* first, so the early exploration was solo, beginning with the Lioness—which led to the purchase of a few more toys.

I still haven't figured out how to make one of them work well for me, and I've continued to be afraid of the other. I think it might be time to clear some time on my calendar, charge it up, and see what the fuss is all about.

All in the name of research!

CHAPTER 17

PARENTING

A note on this chapter: wherever you are with kids, this is a judgment-free zone.

If you've chosen not to have kids, I commend you for your choice. If you've not been able to have children and wanted them, I'm sorry. If you have a unique parenting situation, I respect your challenges and that my situation may be very different from yours. Enjoy this section or skip it, but please feel free to choose what's best for you.

There's nothing to truly prepare you for parenting.

Especially for women.

We can't catch a break! Whether it's choosing to have kids, not to have kids, not being *able* to have kids, the number of kids we have, working from home, or staying home with the kids. Society seems to have an opinion on all of these, and there's no winning formula. Everyone's a critic. Even other women.

My husband and I decided when we got married that he would be the one to stay home with the kids because I had greater earning potential. Before we had our son, he was a police officer and enjoyed his work, so our kids ended up in daycare. Between rotating shifts, mandatory overtime, and court appearances, my husband's schedule was unpredictable and constantly changing. I became the one primarily responsible for caring for our children and the household while working full time.

It was challenging (and unsustainable), and I never felt as if I managed any of it very well. There was little time for me to take care of me. Our marriage suffered.

One night we were out for dinner on a very rare date night, and we had a serious conversation about our life, the kids, and our marriage.

"Maybe I should quit my job," he said.

Slightly panicked, but open to the idea, I did some rough calculations on a cocktail napkin and determined that we could make the finances work. The options were that, or get divorced.

Later that month, he left the police force and has been home with the kids for over twelve years. We are very lucky to have that option. The burden of being financially responsible for the household isn't too heavy for me, but I have and do work a lot, which means I've missed baseball games and back-to-school nights. My son recently said he felt I abandoned him during his formative years. *Hello! You had a parent at home . . . your dad. It's not like I was never home or traveled a lot.*

Now that the kids are teenagers, I try to be around in the morning. I want them to know that even though I've worked a lot, I'm there for them when they need me. Especially with the big stuff . . . but also, for the small stuff.

There's no perfect balance or formula. If we strive to succeed professionally, we make compromises personally. If we stay at home, we're sacrificing an ambitious part of ourselves and may have had other dreams put on the back burner.

If you're parenting little ones in your forties and fifties, honestly, I don't know how you're doing it! I commend you. They're little for a long time before they start to resent you—so hug them. Squeeze them. Let them play with Play-Doh (hate it) and glitter (love it), and don't miss out on a nap just because the house isn't clean. Pretending there's some illusion of control is delusional. (I'm one of the delusional ones, by the way.)

If you have teenagers or tweens, this is the time to focus on self-care to preserve your sanity. As we go through our midlife puberty while our kids are going through adolescent puberty, oh Lordy, there are a lot of hormones flying!

And if your kids have already flown the coop, I've heard that once the kids move out, it doesn't get any easier . . . it just changes.

Bottom line: none of us know what we're doing, and we're all figuring it out along the way.

We're raising a tech-savvy and conscientious generation, who are looking to do good in the world, so all is not lost. We have a lot to celebrate and be proud of, despite how difficult the parenting journey seems to be.

PARENTING A TEENAGER, PART 1: NOTHING PREPARES YOU FOR IT

I lost sleep recently one night because I was worried about my son not getting into some colleges he wanted. Then two nights later, I worried because he'd waited until the last minute to write the first draft of his senior thesis and pulled an all-nighter. He had 102.9% in AP Biology and a C in AP Calculus.

The last year has been especially challenging with a new newly minted adult and a fourteen-year-old. I embody the phrase, "I am a parent; therefore, I drink."

Our son was getting ready to turn eighteen when he, in all seriousness, asked that we be his friends and not his parents. Wow! He has friends who give him a free place to live, food, college education, a Jeep, subsidize his car insurance, and medical care?

I wish I had these kinds of friends.

We're negotiating what it means to be an adult living in our household until he goes to college. I've told him that courtesy and safety are my primary areas of concern. I know he just wants to do what he wants whenever the fuck he wants. I can relate.

I want the same thing too.

PARENTING A TEENAGER, PART 2: WE ARE NOT OUR PARENTS

My parents were very strict when I was in high school, but my husband's parents were incredibly permissive. Since I rebelled and Zeke turned out just fine, we've opted for a more permissive parenting style that includes an *attempt* at continuous communication.

We have encouraged our son to go out and experience things in high school largely because if he doesn't, he will encounter them for the first time in college. Things could go sideways with sudden exposure to massive freedom. I'd rather he be closer to home when he does stupid things for the first time.

We don't condone underage drinking but know it happens, so we have conversations about it. We've encouraged him in sports, school, drama, and jobs. By all accounts, we have been incredibly understanding, which makes it all the more difficult to deal with his resentment, hatred, and other negative feelings. With my being in the crosshairs every single time, it's downright painful.

It feels as if time is running out to make sure he is in a good mental space for college. Isn't this one of the goals of parenting a teenager? Give them freedom to learn in a safe environment, and equip them with effective tools to be safe later in life when we aren't there to guide them.

I'm already worrying about him as he heads off to college. There's a litany of questions running through my already-busy brain. Will he have enough money? Will he make good friends? Will he make good choices (or at least not totally stupid and harmful decisions)? Will he figure out who he is? Will he begin to prepare himself for his future? Will he reach out to someone, or to us, if he needs help?

This is what we've told him we want for him from his college experience:

- Learn how to think critically.
- Have fun.
- Get a better idea of who he is and what he wants out of this life.
- Not get anyone pregnant.
- Make friends.
- Not get seriously hurt physically or emotionally.
- Not cause physical or emotional hurt to anyone else.
- Get a college degree within four years.
- Figure out what his next step is going to be.

We realize that it isn't about us anymore (not like it ever really was), and how he behaves isn't a reflection on how well we've raised him or prepared him for the world. At this point, it's all about us letting go. Funny how that theme keeps cropping up in midlife, isn't it?

Easier said than done.

As we send our not-so-little ones off into the bigger world, a gap opens up. We can let our other kids (if we have them) fill this gap or choose to spend this newfound time and freedom on ourselves. I vote for self-care, a new hobby, or a new activity.

Better yet, how about all three?

SPEAKING OF LETTING GO

Delusionally, I thought I was in good shape for Adam's senior year of high school. I hadn't really thought about all the *lasts*. Consequently, there have been moments when I've totally lost it.

Seeing him in a tux for his senior photos, and not being allowed in the photo-shoot room, must have triggered something because *bam!* Like a sucker punch to the gut, I lost it. Didn't see that coming.

Same thing happened when I was going through thousands of pictures for a dedicated yearbook page (he was mortified, but I don't care). I found myself taking deep breaths and drying tears.

There was another day when I started crying in the kitchen. I don't even know what started it. Adam gave me a hug when I said to him, "I am so excited for you . . . and yet I know I will miss you. I like who you've become, and I enjoy spending time with you."

He laughed, and that was the end of the special mother-son bonding moment.

Through this, I've realized I'm mourning the loss of the little boy who squeezed me tight, said "I love you," and shared his thoughts. Now, we hardly see him. He rarely wants to be in the same room with us (unless he's bingeing *Game of Thrones*), let alone talk to us.

We spend so much time focused on our kids, their emotional well-being, and making sure they're well prepared, that we don't take care of our emotional health. Just as they're transitioning, so are *we*. Transitions are hard work! They bring up all sorts of emotions and insecurities. As our kids move on, so must we.

Have you seen any advertisements or recommendations for mamas to get help during these transitions? Nope! Me neither (now there's a business opportunity). The focus seems to be on getting the kids safely out of the nest and keeping them out.

We often forget to breathe and allow ourselves to *feel* the complex emotions as our kids move on. We need to be able to feel all the feels, and some of them hurt, like punch-you-in-the-stomach, can't-breathe, runny-nose, ugly-crying-face hurt.

And that's okay.

Pass me the tissues.

GEN Z . . . THEY ARE THEM

Depending on the research, 35-50% of Gen Z's know a nonbinary person.

Nonbinary people do not identify with a masculine or feminine gender. They are not she/her or he/him; they prefer they/them pronouns. Where we live, this percentage is probably much higher.

My second child, Rei (born as our daughter, Rachel) identifies as nonbinary. I struggle to use *they* instead of *she* largely because I'm not ready to let go of her as my daughter, and I think she is still trying to figure out who she really is.

We have a few friends with kids like this, mostly children born female (also referred to as cis-female or assigned female at birth). None of us saw any evidence of this dysphoria before the age of twelve or thirteen.

We are seeing more evidence of Gen Z rejecting the rigid view of gender roles. Gender exploration is common in this generation. We're also seeing a rejection of gender labels; these kids don't want to be put in a box. Some kids in this age group can't face the idea of growing up to be a woman because of societal challenges. At the same time, we're seeing a wave of gender-identity experimentation. Suddenly, it seems, no one is cisgender anymore.[35]

I've often thought about all of this over the last two years as we've gone through this journey with Rei. She didn't ever say she wanted to be a boy, and she didn't reject being a girl. I really do think, as I read in the same article I quoted above, that she saw something online and that led to something else, and eventually she found answers that made sense but didn't necessarily explain everything.

At fourteen, Rei is continuing to find who she is and will hopefully continue to find support from others and, more importantly, strength from within, to continue to evolve into adulthood as a person.

Rei is a product of how we raised her. Be who you are. Love who you love. Accept others where they are. Fight for the right for others to do the same.

SHARENTING AND PRIVACY

I confess, I've been posting pictures of my kids and my life on Facebook for over a decade.

I don't share as much anymore, but the damage is done. My kids hate it. They groan if they see me doing it. Fortunately, they haven't sued me for it (I've seen a few reported cases of this).

With recent revelations around privacy issues, many of us are choosing to be on some of these platforms less. It's hard to give it up cold turkey, though.

I've witnessed our Gen Z kids rebelling against parents oversharing on social media, also called sharenting (sharing + parenting). They're using apps like SnapChat, where they can make text and photos disappear and WhatsApp, which allows them to create closed, intimate groups. They can be selective about who sees what on social media. They have multiple Instagram accounts—one private and one public.

While they may not use complete sentences or even words, and they may love emojis and GIFs instead of actual language, I felt better after hearing from Dr. Eliza Filby that this generation drinks less, has less sex, and has fewer tattoos. They crave human interaction, prioritize mental health, and embrace differences and naturalness. So, what am I really going to see in their feeds?

Some things I think I'm better off not knowing.

MENTAL HEALTH AND ANXIETY

Both of our kids are in therapy.

Friends and acquaintances ask us for recommendations for mental health professionals and about our experiences with our kids all the time.

The American Psychological Association released a report in October 2018 stating that members of Gen Z—people born between 1995 and 2012—reported the worst mental health of any generation.[36]

This isn't surprising, given that a report in 2018 from Blue Cross Blue Shield showed a 33% increase in clinical depression diagnoses since 2013.[37] Mass shootings, worries about climate change, separation and deportation of immigrant and migrant families, and sexual harassment and assault reports top the charts in terms of national news topics, contributing to stress and anxiety for Gen Z. This doesn't even take into account social media and social pressures.

The good news is that Gen Z, on average, is more likely to discuss mental health issues and seek help.

Colleges are struggling to keep up with the demand. A number of them are trying to find alternative ways to reduce wait time, provide consistent therapy appointments where the students are at and without stigma, and help them build skills and reduce anxiety. Some are performing incoming freshmen surveys and assessments.

Programs helping kids transition into college after they've dropped out are on the rise. We have several friends who have kids who seemed to be ready, went off to college, and were back home by the second semester. In the case of two of the boys, neither found *their people*. One will start back at a local university in the fall. The other one now has a full-time job and may pick up at the local junior college in the fall. Or not.

Several of my son's friends have expressed concern about being able to handle college after seeing some of their friends move back home their freshman year. If they're questioning it, does that show awareness, or a crack in confidence?

These kinds of transitions are hard on our kids. I didn't find *my people* when I was a freshman, and I moved back home to finish up at the local university. It didn't occur to me to seek out help. Did these other kids ask for help? I've been encouraging my son to keep a line open with his therapist just in case he needs help when he's at school. He says he can handle it.

For my own sanity, I am choosing to have confidence in my kids and hope that they will continue to ask for help if they need it. I've also extended to some of their friends the same option—if they're stuck or need help, they can call me, no questions asked.

Who am I kidding? I'll ask them a ton of questions, but I won't judge or criticize.

ALL IS NOT LOST

Have you ever heard another parent comment about how well behaved or polite or witty your kid is, and you wonder who they're talking about?

As I was doing research on Gen Z, it felt good to step back and view this generation at a macro level and see how impressive they are. We must be doing *something* right as Gen X parents because Gen Z kids are already looking for ways to positively impact the world. This generation saw Malala Yousafzai win the Nobel Peace Prize at eighteen. They're generous and self-aware. Gen Z has been listening. I think they're more prepared than we might expect.

Gen Z kids are entrepreneurial and want to invent and make their own things. They want to buy from companies with socially responsible missions. Because they are so connected with technology, and they are able to absorb a lot of information, they are easily able to fact-check and see through lies and past bad behavior.

I am more optimistic about my kids and their futures right now than I've been in a long time, but maybe that's the wine talking.

TAKING THE CONTROLS

— How is my role as a parent shifting?
— Am I paying enough attention to my own needs?
— What do I need as my role changes?

BRIEFING NOTES

....
....
....
....
....
....
....
....
....
....
....
....
....
....
....
....
....
....
....

CHAPTER 18

MONEY AND
FINANCIAL FREEDOM

Midlife is the time for us women to get our financial houses in order and address any issues we might have with money, whether it's earning, saving, investing, spending, or our own self-worth.

Research shows that women's salaries peak in their forties, while men's peak in their fifties. More women tend to lose or leave their jobs in their fifties while men experience this in their sixties. We're at a financial disadvantage from the very beginning, making only $0.78 (or less) to a man's dollar.

In some cases, our relationship with money is the issue. In other cases, it's the worry about money or lack thereof. Some of us have built up successful careers, and we're asking if our salaries are worth the corporate battles. Some women tire of the constant fight for equality and visibility. No matter what we do, our opportunities aren't the same as for our male counterparts.

Some women realize that they want to create something new, but they have financial obligations in the form of mortgages, college tuition, and/or helping aging parents. Letting go of some sense of security to pursue something new is daunting.

Then there's the cost of healthcare.

Many women in the U.S. stay in unsatisfying jobs or positions because they need the health benefits. They end up choosing stability over happiness.

Added to all that, not all of us have healthy relationships with money. I, for one, am wondering when I will stop worrying about money. When will I feel like I have enough? Am I alone in worrying about having enough to take care of me and my family?

Is this fear irrational?

According to a terrifying 2016 study from the National Institute on Retirement Security, women were found to be 80% more likely than men to be impoverished in retirement. Women tend to live longer than men. We will also need more money to last longer to meet daily life expenses, and are more likely to need long-term healthcare because of our longevity.[38]

So, what is a girl to do?

All is not lost. Between assessing, learning, smart planning, asking for some help, and taking risks, we can slay financial demons and create paths to a healthier financial future.

WE NEED TO TALK ABOUT MONEY

Why don't we talk about money?

So many of us weren't raised to be financially literate. Even with the exposure I had working for my dad's accounting firm, I still managed to make bad decisions and ended up with credit card debt in college. My parents gave me a personal loan at a lower interest rate than standard, and I paid it all back and learned about amortization schedules.

Sallie Krawcheck, founder of Ellevest, regularly talks about how women don't take enough risks with money and, compounded, will not make as much as men over our lifetimes. We don't work as long as men, generally, and some of us take time off for pregnancy, childbirth, and childrearing. And did I mention that women tend to live longer and take care of more people in their lifetime? This creates quite the financial quagmire.

We also don't get exposed to the same financial and investing opportunities. When Sallie was working on Wall Street, the men she worked with would pass a hat around to raise funds for a buddy to make an investment. She was never included, and she was an *investment banker*. Even if we are financially literate, and in the right place where the deals are happening, the deals still aren't made available to us.

So, why aren't we talking about this? Are we afraid of looking dumb? Are we afraid to face the reality of our financial situations? Do we not know where to start? Or is it a combination of all of these?

I talk with some of my friends about finances in the abstract, never mentioning actual numbers. Even that feels awkward and somewhat shameful. If you are like me, you were raised with the understanding that talking about money was considered gauche and impolite. Just as we need to talk about our physical and mental health, we should be talking about our financial health so we can normalize our fears, dreams, needs, wants, and plans for our financial futures.

RELATIONSHIP WITH MONEY

I grew up solidly middle class, and it wasn't always that way.

My parents were very young when they got married in San Francisco. My sister and I were *oops* babies, and my parents weren't financially ready to have two of us. My dad worked for Arthur Andersen as an accountant and understood the value of hard work. He worked hard to provide us with a financially secure childhood.

We moved to a San Francisco suburb when I was six months old. A few years later, we moved to the next town over, where my brother was born. When I started first grade, my parents moved to a bigger house thirty minutes away, which is where I grew up. My dad told my mom they would live there for two years, three tops. They sold the house and moved thirty years later.

I always remember having enough. My dad worked all the time—I'm pretty sure I inherited his workaholic tendencies. When he wasn't working, he was paying bills or reading stacks of *Wall Street Journals* in the hot tub. My parents didn't argue over money, but Mom did use it against Dad.

One day when I was a freshman in high school and my mom was angry with my dad, she announced that we were going shopping. We had a dance coming up, and my mom always made sure we had new outfits for every dance. We found a complicated outfit that I loved but was ridiculously expensive. My mom announced, "We'll take it!" Then she took me shoe shopping.

Shopping was always fun when my dad pissed my mom off, but it didn't set me up for a healthy relationship with money. Recently, I discovered I have a tendency to sabotage my own financial well-being.

My mom never really cared about money. She values people, causes, and experiences. My dad, on the other hand, values money over all else. He makes it, invests it, and prides himself on his financial success without flaunting it.

Like my dad, I make money, invest it, and pride myself on financial success, but I also share my mother's values. There are occasions when I'm pissed off at something and will say, "Fuck it!" Then, I'll spend money on something in retaliation, usually at my own expense.

Literally and figuratively.

I believe my mom felt powerless in her relationship with my dad on occasion and weaponized money. She probably didn't do this consciously, but it made an impression on me. With this awareness, I hope to create better habits. When I catch myself throwing all caution to the wind, I can stop, breathe, and ask myself a few questions.

Am I buying this because I need it?

How will I feel after I spend this money?

Will I regret it?

Am I trying to make myself feel better only to have it make me feel worse later?

With awareness, we create the space for action and change.

HEY LADIES, INVESTING IS AN OPTION

Even after all the years that I invested based on my dad's recommendations and watched my dad sit on the boards of startups, I didn't know that angel investing was an option for me. This is one of the reasons I am such a vocal proponent for women in angel investing.

Women can influence, financially, the products and services that end up in our world. Men make up 92% of venture capitalists, which means they are the ones deciding which startups are funded and at what level.

Men don't tend to fund things that benefit women. Seventy to eighty percent of venture capitalists are white men. Not only do they not recognize their privilege, they don't realize there are opportunities to invest in products and services for consumers who don't look or act like them (sometimes called pattern matching).

Women can use money as a path to power.

Jane Fonda and Lily Tomlin, who have been friends for years, conducted an interview together where Jane reminded the audience that if women came together, we could be an impressive and massive force for change. They're both amazingly accomplished women and impressive advocates. Men haven't been doing that great of a job, if you ask me, and it's time to swing a bit more toward the feminine. Not only do we exist, but we have different needs and wants.

Yep, down with the patriarchy.

Women make 75-85% of consumer purchasing decisions and over 85% of household healthcare spending decisions. Could you imagine our influence if we used that spending power in our buying decisions? Product managers and marketers wouldn't be able to ignore our wants and needs.

CREATING A RAINY-DAY FUND (AKA, A FUCK YOU FUND)

Money is power. It's also freedom.

As we reach an age where we're no longer willing to put up with corporate crap or want to explore new territory, a financial cushion helps. For some, this may be easier than for others. Women generally make more conservative decisions when under stress at a time when a bit more risk is worth taking.

Sallie Krawcheck says in the Covey Club podcast that, "You need to create a rainy-day fund so you can walk away, and be prepared if someone walks away from you or asks you to leave. You need to have the guts to walk away."

Others have referred to it as the *Fuck You Fund*. Whatever you call it, this fund allows you to be financially prepared.

Books and many articles have been written on the subject of how women can begin to take control over their financial futures. I'm not talking about the articles that tell women to stop buying shoes and lattes. Yes, we may need to sacrifice or make compromises in the short term to begin to establish this fund, if we haven't already done so. I don't deny this. But we also need to consider taking some financial risks to create greater financial opportunity. That will begin to make up for the financial gaps that most likely exist in our lives.

We must acknowledge the financial gaps and then be intentional about filling them.

CREATING YOUR OWN FINANCIAL PATH

Many women are starting their own businesses to have greater control over their schedules and their paychecks. Fortunately, it's easier than ever. For some, this is the only path forward after leaving the workforce to raise children or being laid off after fifty. (Ageism is real!)

It takes creativity and gumption to launch a business, but the rewards can be worth the extra risk and effort, as some of the women I interviewed recounted in their stories.

CHECKING IN WITH A PROFESSIONAL

Chrissy spent the majority of her professional career working for large consumer goods companies in a heavily male environment, all while consistently exceeding expectations. She always saw the competition and the *good ol' boys club* as inspiring challenges . . . until it became annoying and frustrating. Her performance couldn't beat the bro club.

In her late forties, she left the corporate environment and moved into consulting for seven years, at which point a personal experience drove her to solve a medical problem other midlife women were experiencing, but most likely not talking about.

She researched to prove the market existed and validated her hypothesis, at which point she consulted with her financial advisor, Martha. She was fifty-five at the time.

"Martha told me that I could easily take $100,000 and a year to get the startup off the ground. We concluded that if I wasn't able to make it work, it was back to corporate for me. I had no real safety net to speak of and no spouse's income to fall back on."

She was methodical and disciplined in her approach and leveraged her significant experience and network. She brought advisors in to fill gaps and prepared a business plan with a solid vision to get investors on board.

"Every day is hard, and every day I have doubts. It's been over six years since I started the company, and my business is thriving. I'm not going back to corporate any time soon, if ever. I look at the trade-offs and was happy to make them. I never saw it as sacrifice, and I don't regret any of the decisions. I have $500,000 of my own money in the business, so I'm working hard for my investors and for me. If this doesn't end up working out, I'll be working forever, but that's OK."

She firmly believes in trading something comfortable for something more uncomfortable to really make a difference and make progress. She says, "I'm willing to pay the price."

SCRATCHING AN ENTREPRENEURIAL ITCH

Jayne spent decades in higher education. Her professional life felt like a series of experiments. She was months away from retirement when she decided to follow a hunch and start up a tech company with a co-founder. When we spoke, she said, "I saw an opportunity and was very familiar with the pain point. I'd grown comfortable with taking risks and knew that if the venture failed, I could take retirement at age sixty."

She was almost fifty at the time. Her wife had a great job that provided for their family, which made it easier to take the leap.

"I left a secure job with an opportunity for retirement in order to pursue a bigger dream and a bigger vision. I wasn't done contributing to the world, and I continue to work every day to make a difference, not only as a female founder/CEO of a tech startup, but also in the education space.

"I learned the hard way that once you go down a path, it's often difficult to turn around. You just have to work through it. And everything has taken longer than we expected. At the same time, I've been surprised by a lot on this journey."

I asked her if she would have stayed in her old job and retired on schedule if she had the chance to go back, and she said, "No. I would do this all over again. I have the opportunity to create financial freedom for my family. I wouldn't have been able to do that in my old job."

OUT WITH THE OLD, IN WITH THE NEW

Roxanne had been a tech consultant for over fifteen years and was struggling to take her business to the next level. She'd been working with a business coach to help her find her way and just couldn't get it right.

While at a women's conference, it hit her; she knew exactly what she wanted to do.

"I wrote the business plan during the conference and planned to use my existing business to fund my new venture. I was so excited and inspired. It felt so right."

But there was a catch.

She needed to keep the old business going because she didn't have enough savings to fire her clients and spend all of her time building the new business. "It was frustrating," she said. "For the longest time, I felt like I lived in two worlds. Because I didn't have a strong financial safety net, I had to be cautious about building the new business *and* still stay focused on the old business. I really wanted to be 100% devoted to building the new one. My heart wasn't in the old work."

She gradually started shifting her focus and eventually reached the point where the new business became the priority. "When it finally shifted in my head, I started making much more progress on the new business. It started evolving much more quickly."

She is no longer chasing work for her old business and is putting her faith in the new venture. She knows she needs to give it more attention.

"I'm more stressed financially, but it's a risk I am willing to take. I know I am doing the right thing. I'm dipping into my retirement plan, and, to save money, I am doing things on a shoestring budget. I have to be very creative. But it's worth it. The opportunities and the revenue are there."

CREATING A NEW FINANCIAL REALITY WITH MULTIPLE INCOME STREAMS

Vera left a research position at a prominent research facility to be a stay-at-home mom after the birth of her second child. She'd worked hard toward her Ph.D. and enjoyed her research work but wanted to make sure she was a deliberate parent to her girls. It didn't seem to be an option that her husband stay home . . . it was never discussed.

While she put her own needs and desires on hold, she enjoyed being there for her girls and providing them with a nurturing and stimulating environment.

"I reached a point where I wanted more. I started a flexible job at a local company and discovered that I really liked the coaching part of the work. I thought maybe I could become a life coach."

She took classes and trained to become certified. She wasn't sure that would be enough. "I'd asked my husband for a divorce; then realized I needed to play bigger and make more money to support us."

She started freelancing, then landed a marketing and communication role at a local nonprofit. She uses it to supplement her income and stay relevant. Her path to financial and emotional freedom is becoming clear, and is based on a series of intentional steps, serendipity, risk, and hard work. Her serpentine path makes sense as she looks back.

Having multiple revenue streams means that if one dries up, we have others to stave off financial disaster. This makes even more sense as we age. Because of sexism, we don't make as much money as men during our lifetimes. Because of ageism, research shows we are let go from corporate jobs sooner than men.

A girl has got to have a plan.

PLANNING FOR YOUR FINANCIAL FUTURE

One of the statistics on the Ellevest website surprised me: women over fifty were most likely to tell them that they never talk to anyone about financial advice.[39]

Is it because we don't know who to trust? Or are we afraid of what we'll learn? Or that we think it's too expensive, and we don't think we can afford it? Something else?

My dad consulted with us on tax planning and investing, and we benefited from his advice. Then we started paying more attention to the investments and began to disagree based on values. Now, like the women in the survey, I no longer have someone to talk to about retirement, taxes, and general financial planning.

Now is the time for us to put together our team of trusted

advisors to talk about our life plans, our financial needs, and getting a plan in place. Women retire with two-thirds less money than men and live six to eight years longer! We cannot emphasize these statistics enough. We can get recommendations from friends on ideal resources and do some reference checking to create a solid and reliable financial team.

If you're in your forties or fifties and had kids, you're most likely getting close to having, or already have, the kids out of the house. Your life is getting close to being your own again (unless you're also taking care of aging parents, in which case there are added complexities). If you don't have kids, your life is already your own, which means you are a step ahead.

This is the perfect time to put on your dream goggles and think about your future in retirement. If you're already retired, good for you! I'd still double-check your plans and resources against your dreams and make sure you are all set!

I laughed out loud when I read in "5 Smart Money Moves to Make in Your 50s" that retirement is "potentially only a decade or so away."[40] Our generation will not be retiring at sixty or sixty-five. We'll be working well into our seventies. Think about it. If we're going to live up to or past ninety, is it reasonable to expect a thirty-year retirement period and have it effectively funded?

Not likely.

Especially for those of us Gen Xers who have been through several recessions and market corrections.

That same article suggests that we dream up our ideal lifestyle and then price it out. Then we can calculate our required annual income. This activity can trigger all sorts of emotional and psychological demons, so I recommend having some sort of support system in place—preferably not alcoholic.

While my husband insists that we will never move (and we live in a modest house as it is, so downsizing won't be necessary), I think a fair bit of travel is in my future, including spending part of every year in my own *pied-à-terre* in Paris. With or without him—his choice!

Most of us aren't trained tax and financial planning professionals. We require assistance. Having trusted advisors when performing these dreaming-and-planning exercises is very helpful. They can help us take our dreams, put plans together to support those dreams, align ourselves, correct on a regular basis, and make our dreams a reality.

If you already have a plan in place, this is the time to revisit it and make sure you're still on track.

This isn't the time to put your head in the sand and hope someone else will take care of this. Know what you have, what you owe, what you earn, and what you spend. We don't live in the 1950s (contrary to what the patriarchy would like us to believe). As a result, we have as much of a responsibility to own our financial situation as our partner (if we have one).

While it's better to have a financial safety net before making significant changes, that's not always realistic or practical. You don't always have the choice. The important thing is to not let money get in the way of pursuing your midlife dreams and passions. Having a plan in place is better than no plan, but no plan will ever be bulletproof.

TAKING THE CONTROLS

— Is my financial house in order?
— When do I want to retire?
— What is my ideal lifestyle at retirement?

BRIEFING NOTES

CHAPTER 19

FLIGHT PLAN

PILOTING AN AIRCRAFT VS.
PILOTING YOUR LIFE

When I became a helicopter pilot, someone asked me why I chose helicopters over airplanes. I responded with attitude, "Because anyone can fly an airplane."

After I got my helicopter pilot's license, I had every intention of getting what is called a fixed-wing add-on so I could fly airplanes. There's a general rule that if you want to see things, you take a helicopter. If you want to go places, you take an airplane. It's exhausting and expensive to fly helicopters, and it doesn't make sense to fly them long distances (or at least not the ones I fly).

I logged a few hours in the cockpit of a Cessna 172 (four-seater airplane) with a flight instructor and very quickly realized I wouldn't be able to spend enough time training and flying to be safe in multiple types of aircraft. There are some basic helicopter pilot attitudes and maneuvers that will kill you in a plane and vice versa. It's not worth the risk for me right now, but I envision that one day I will give airplanes a try again. This will most likely be when the kids are out of college and I have more time and discretionary income to fly helicopters and airplanes more frequently.

Regardless of the aircraft, pilots are responsible for performing certain tasks to be safe and effective in the air and on the ground.

Before every flight, before I even start the helicopter, I:

- Check in with myself and make sure I am feeling good and not tired, sick, distracted, or under the influence of medications or alcohol.

- Check the aircraft's logbooks for any issues, including recent maintenance.
- Plan my route.
- Get an official weather briefing.
- Check for any flight restrictions in the flight area, including airports.
- Calculate how much fuel I will need and whether I need to make any stops for refueling.
- Do a weight and balance to make sure the helicopter can handle the load, including fuel.
- Make backup plans in the event that the route or the airports have a problem (otherwise called *preparing for diversions*).
- Get familiar with frequencies, airspace, and airports.
- Perform a thorough preflight of the helicopter to make sure it is airworthy.
- Make a go, no-go decision.
- Get myself set up in the cockpit with my charts, headset, quick reference guides, and checklists.
- Brief and prepare my passengers.

As I thought about how to wrap up some of the major themes of the book, I got to thinking about how analogous our midlife journey is to my pre-flight activities, flying, and post-flight checks.

- We are living our journey.
- We have to know where we are starting and familiarize ourselves with our starting point.
- We need to identify where we want to go, or at least the first stop.
- We need to know who is coming with us and what their roles are. Are they passengers? Co-pilots? Other?

- We need to figure out what resources and information we need to get to our destination.
- We need to make sure we are healthy and aware of any limitations, and then operate within those boundaries.
- We need to take care of ourselves and perform regular self-care and maintenance.
- To perform optimally, we need to do what we can to reduce drag, create lift, and leave unnecessary baggage behind.
- Once we are on our way, we continue to make decisions, correct course, and stay actively involved in piloting our personal journeys.
- Once we reach our intended destination (or diverted location), we check in and see how everything went and see what we can learn from the experience.

FLIGHT PLAN

If you are wondering where the hell to start after getting this far in the book, have no fear. It can be overwhelming to determine where to start because there's so much opportunity in midlife.

Yes, I said, opportunity.

Our age doesn't limit us; only our imaginations and willingness to do the work (and maybe some financial constraints).

I provided some questions at the end of each chapter (*Taking the Controls*) to get you thinking. You can always start with those if you haven't already done so.

It's impossible to create a prescriptive approach for *all* women because each of you lovely ladies gets to create your own life based on your own dreams, likes, dislikes, and experiences. Kind of like the *Choose Your Own Adventure* books we read when we were kids.

But how to get you started? The answer came to me in the dead of night as I struggled to get back to sleep. I was so excited (and afraid

I would forget) that I turned on the light and wrote it down and sketched out a picture.

This book is all about being the pilots in our own lives . . . so what we need is a flight plan.

Be thoughtful and intentional in your planning, and enjoy your journey!

Check out the website www.PilotingYourLife.com to create your own personal Flight Plan.

FLIGHT PLAN

PILOT NAME _____ AGE _____

STARTING POINT _____ DESTINATION _____

      ❑ SET DESTINATION   ❑ EXPLORATORY FLIGHT

PERIOD OF TIME ❑ <1 YEAR ❑ 1-2 YEARS ❑ 2-5 YEARS ❑ 5-10 YEARS

CHECKPOINTS	EST. DURATION	ETA	PRIORITY

REQUIRED RESOURCES	
TIME	
$$$	
PEOPLE	
OTHER	

HEALTH CHECK
❑ SELF CARE
❑ MINDFULNESS
❑ SUPPORT
❑ EXERCISE
❑ NUTRITION
❑ WATER
❑ OTHER

DRAG TO BE ELIMINATED
❑ _____
❑ _____
❑ _____
❑ _____
❑ _____
❑ _____
❑ _____

OBSTACLES TO AVOID ❑ _____ ❑ _____ ❑ _____

NOTES: _____

_____

_____

CHAPTER 20

IT'S ALL RIGHT
IN THE END

I t's not the end; it's just the beginning.

Older women are finally being recognized and celebrated for their greatness. I see new articles nearly every week showcasing the accomplishments of well-known women like Ruth Bader Ginsburg, Sonia Sotomayor, Billie Jean King, Hillary Rodham Clinton, Maxine Waters, Nancy Pelosi, Helen Mirren, Glenn Close, Meryl Streep, Jane Fonda, Lily Tomlin, Ellen DeGeneres, Oprah Winfrey, and Elizabeth Warren.

These inspirational role models prove that age needn't limit or negatively define us. These women, and many more who are less well known, are demonstrating the value of the experience, wisdom, and perspective that can only come with age. Finally, we can embrace aging and all the goodness that comes with it.

We can let go of what was and create what will be. For us.

We may not find it the first time, or even the tenth time, but that's where all the fun is: in the exploration, the creation, the learning, and the growing. Even if it feels as if many of our firsts are behind us, there are plenty ahead of us, assuming we are willing to take charge and create our own opportunities.

One day, I may play in a real poker tournament for the very first time. It's terrifying and daunting to think about, but I'll never know what the experience is like unless I give it a try. For you, it will likely be something completely different.

Maybe it's traveling to a foreign country by yourself and exploring on your own.

Maybe it's going to a yoga class for the first time and making it all the way through to shavasana. (Trust me, it's worth it.)

Maybe it's going back to school to pursue a new career or hobby.

Maybe it's writing a book or a screenplay.

Maybe it's getting divorced or getting married or deciding that you want to be alone for a while.

Maybe you have no idea what it will be, but you'll give a few things a try and see what comes up.

It's OK to be afraid of the unknown and still step into it.

It's OK to fail and try again with new knowledge and information. Or to try something else completely different.

It's OK to be who you are, unapologetically. Don't shrink. The world needs your brilliance, your experience, and your perspective.

Be bold, my friends. It's your time.

Take the controls, and be the pilot in your own life.

ABOUT THE
AUTHOR

Terri Hanson Mead is a commercially rated helicopter pilot in the San Francisco Bay Area. She's passionate about encouraging women to live their best lives, free of barriers and restrictions.

Terri has always lived boldly and is known for inspiring others to do the same. She recognizes that while she has a strong internal compass and has defined her life's vision, some women, as they enter midlife in their forties, struggle with navigating this uncharted territory. She seeks to be their guide, the sister they may not have, who will cheer them on and urge them to step boldly into this next phase of their lives.

She wants midlife to be seen as an opportunity for exploration and expansion, full of the greatest of adventures. She's unwavering in her desire to normalize the conversations around midlife changes for women.

Terri has been married for over twenty-three years and is a mother to two teenagers, an entrepreneur, active angel investor, startup advisor, expert witness, podcaster, writer, and advocate for *all* women.

You can learn more at www.TerriHansonMead.com. Follow her on Twitter and Instagram @terrihansonmead, and sign up for the Piloting Your Life newsletter on the Piloting Your Life website at www.PilotingYourLife.com.

APPENDIX 1
CREW CHATS

THE WHAT

I have a vision where all women everywhere feel loved, supported, and inspired to live their best lives.

We can't do this alone.

I'm often surprised by the women who seem to have it all together, or appear to have a ton of friends, but have no one to talk to about midlife—or anything else, for that matter.

We could all use a flight crew (or two or three!) as we navigate our lives. What if we scheduled regular times to meet up and have conversations around provocative midlife topics? And what if we included some education with those conversations?

This is where Crew Chats come into play.

Think of it as Table Topics but just for us midlife women.

I see this as a group of four to five (primarily) women getting together every week, every month, or every other month over snacks and bubbly (alcoholic or otherwise) to talk about what we never talk about. These can be women you want to get to know better . . . or ones you already know really well and want to maintain a strong connection with.

Pick a Crew Chief for each Crew Chat to lead the conversation and pose the questions. Feel free to come up with your own based on what you've read in the news, a pain (or pleasure) point in your life, or just plain curiosity.

I've put together some questions to get your crew started. Find more at www.PilotingYourLife.com. Sign up for the Piloting Your Life newsletter on the website to get new questions and research in your email box each month.

THE WHY

Solid and deep friendships are a key to happiness.

It takes time and commitment to build these relationships, and a lot of us haven't made friendships a priority. We may find ourselves a little isolated and alone. We may think we're connecting on social media, but there's nothing like connecting in person.

Our Crews can help us normalize the conversation about everything from perimenopause to mental health, sex, divorce, money, and legal matters. As women, we shouldn't be afraid or embarrassed to talk about any of these things, regardless of how we were raised and socialized.

As I was searching for the perfect quote to end this section, I came across a blog post that struck a nerve with me.

The author, Angi, said, "What I'm seeing, in my world, are a lot of women going it alone, afraid to share their inner demons, not wanting to be a burden, and therefore not having the energy to be supportive to others."[41]

I don't want to be a burden on anyone else, and I know other women who feel this way too. For those of us who can relate, we *really* need time with friends and Crew Chats.

We all learn and grow from our interactions with our friends, and I think Crew Chats can be a great way to build your life crew, make it easier to talk about taboo subjects, and realize you are not alone.

In fact, you're in great company.

CREW CHAT TIPS

- Set a consistent time and place to meet on a regular basis, whether it's weekly (wouldn't that be nice?), monthly, or every other month. This is best done in a comfortable and private place.
- Keep the Crew to four to five. Any bigger and it turns into a party that separates into smaller crews.

- Whatever is said at the Crew table, stays at the Crew table.
- Be supportive, and ask probing questions. Go deep!
- Laughter, tears, anger, and vulnerability are encouraged.

CREW CHAT QUESTIONS TO GET YOU STARTED

- When was the last time you jumped on a trampoline or jumped rope without peeing a little (or a lot)?
- What is one thing you would do now that you couldn't have imagined doing ten years ago?
- How can we appreciate what our bodies do for us?
- What is your superpower?
- What do you feel like you have to let go of in your life and why?
- What do you feel like you have aged out of?
- Describe your last perfect, delicious moment.
- What is your guilty pleasure? Why is it *guilty*?
- How has sex changed for you since you turned thirty-five? Forty-five?
- What sort of death planning have you done?
- Do you have a financial plan? Do you know where your money is?
- What are three things you have always wanted to do?

NOW WHAT?

Gather your Crew, build relationships, and start strengthening connections while busting taboos!

When women support each other, incredible things happen.
—Author unknown.

Appendix 2
IN-FLIGHT RESOURCES

Want to dig deeper into the topics covered in the book? Check out www.PilotingYourLife.com for links to resources to help you on your midlife journey.

While there, sign up for the newsletter for new Crew Chat questions and periodic updates on other valuable information for midlife women.

REFERENCES

Chapter 1

1   Davis, Richard. "Beginnings and Endings and Beginnings." *UUSF*. August 27, 2018. Accessed March 15, 2019. http://www.uusf.org/ single-post/2017/08/27/Beginnings-and-Endings-and-Beginnings.

Chapter 3

2   Warrell, Margie. "Do You Know Your 'Why?' 4 Questions to Find Your Purpose." *Forbes*. October 30, 2013. Accessed April 17, 2019. https://www.forbes.com/sites/margiewarrell/2013/10/30/ know-your-why-4-questions-to-tap-the-power-of-purpose/.

Chapter 4

3   "Menopause: It's Longer, Harder, and Hotter for People of Color." *UpwellBeing*. March 19, 2019. Accessed April 2, 2019. https://www.upwellbeing.com/ menopause-its-longer-harder-and-hotter-for-people-of-color/.

4   "Risk Factors for Heart Disease, from Dr. Sarah Speck." *Genneve*. February 21, 2019. Accessed April 2, 2019. https://genneve.com/ heart-disease-risk-menopause/.

5   Patel, Hemalee. "Understanding and Preventing Alzheimer's in Women." *Lisa Health Blog*. November 23, 2018. Accessed April 2, 2019. https://blog.lisahealth.com/blog/2018/11/23/ understanding-and-preventing-alzheimers-in-women.

6   "Menopause and Mental Health: Finding Yourself in Isolation." *Genneve*. November 7, 2018. Accessed April 2, 2019. https://genneve.com/ social-isolation-menopause-mental-health/.

7   Railton, David. "What Is the Link Between Menopause and Anxiety?" *Medical News Today*. Accessed April 2, 2019. https://www. medicalnewstoday.com/articles/317552.php.

8   "When the Arrival of Menopause Brings Symptoms of
     Depression." *Harvard Health*. May 2018. Accessed April
     2, 2019. https://www.health.harvard.edu/womens-health/
     when-the-arrival-of-menopause-brings-symptoms-of-depression.

9   Patel, Hemalee. "Understanding and Preventing Alzheimer's
     in Women." *Lisa Health Blog*. November 23, 2018. Accessed
     April 2, 2019. https://blog.lisahealth.com/blog/2018/11/23/
     understanding-and-preventing-alzheimers-in-women.

10   Patel, Hemalee. "Understanding and Preventing Alzheimer's
     in Women." *Lisa Health Blog*. November 23, 2018. Accessed
     April 2, 2019. https://blog.lisahealth.com/blog/2018/11/23/
     understanding-and-preventing-alzheimers-in-women.

CHAPTER 5

11   James, Matt, Ph.D. "How Limiting Are Your Decisions?" *Psychology Today*.
     October 7, 2013. Accessed April 3, 2019. https://www.psychologytoday.
     com/us/blog/focus-forgiveness/201310/how-limiting-are-your-decisions.

12   James, Matt, Ph.D. "4 Steps to Release 'Limiting Beliefs' Learned from
     Childhood." *Psychology Today*. November 5, 2013. Accessed April 3, 2019.
     https://www.psychologytoday.com/us/blog/focus-forgiveness/201311/4-
     steps-release-limiting-beliefs-learned-childhood.

13   Stinson, Nicolette. "10 Steps to Develop an Abundance Mindset."
     Chopra Center. Accessed April 3, 2019. www.nicolettestinson.com/
     blog/10-steps-to-develop-an-abundance-mindset.

14   Jimenez, J. "John C. Maxwell: 6 Tips to Develop and
     Model an Abundance Mindset." SUCCESS. March 4,
     2015. Accessed April 3, 2019. https://www.success.com/
     john-c-maxwell-6-tips-to-develop-and-model-an-abundance-mindset/.

15   Richters, Juliet, Richard De Visser, Chris Rissel, and Anthony Smith.
     "Sexual Practices at Last Heterosexual Encounter and Occurrence of
     Orgasm in a National Survey." *Journal of Sex Research*. August 2006.
     Accessed June 19, 2019. https://www.ncbi.nlm.nih.gov/pubmed/17599244.

CHAPTER 7

16   Mueller, Annie. "8 Exercises to Help You Let Go of the Things That No
     Longer Serve You." *Catapult*. January 16, 2018. Accessed April 15, 2019.
     https://catapult.co/community/stories/8-exercises-to-help-you-let-go-of-
     the-things-that-no-longer-serve-you.

17 Bennett, Jessica. *Feminist Fight Club. Portfolio Penguin*, 2017.

18 Hamaui, Daniela. "Why So Many Women Are Trying to Be 'Perfect.'" *Medium*. January 11, 2017. Accessed April 15, 2019. https://medium. com/thrive-global/why-many-women-want-to-be-perfect-85a8df41ae04.

MIRROR MIRROR ON THE WALL

19 Faubion, Stephanie. "Midlife Weight Gain-Sound Familiar? You're Not Alone." MenoPause Blog. January 23, 2018. Accessed April 2, 2019. https://www.menopause.org/for-women/ menopause-take-time-to-think-about-it/consumers/2018/01/23/ midlife-weight-gain-sound-familiar-you-re-not-alone.

CHAPTER 8

20 "Why Do We Grieve?" *Mercy Cremations*. Accessed April 5, 2019. https://mercycremations.com/why-do-we-grieve.html.

CHAPTER 12

21 Nyad, Diana. "Never, Ever Give Up." *TED*. December 2013. Accessed April 13, 2019. https://www.ted.com/talks/ diana_nyad_never_ever_give_up?language=en.

CHAPTER 14

22 Pilossoph, Jackie. "Be Kind to the Perimenopausal Women in Your Life." *Chicago Tribune*. March 6, 2019. Accessed April 10, 2019. https://www.chicagotribune.com/suburbs/ct-ahp-column-love-essentially-tl-0314-story.html.

CHAPTER 15

23 Williams, Alex. "Why Is It Hard to Make Friends Over 30?" *The New York Times*. July 13, 2012. Accessed March 27, 2019. https://www.nytimes.com/2012/07/15/fashion/the-challenge-of-making-friends-as-an-adult.html?mtrref=www.google. com&gwh=E011EB1660A95F1B6094257F18637CC1&gwt=pay.

24 Van De Vyver, Julie and Crisp, Richard. "Crossing Divides: The Friends Who Are Good for Your Brain." *BBC News*. March 2, 2019. Accessed March 3, 2019. https://www.bbc.com/news/uk-47369648.

25 "A Third of American Adults Age 45 and Over Are Lonely, National Survey Finds." *ABC News*. September 25, 2018. Accessed March 27, 2019. https://abcnews.go.com/Health/american-adults-age-45-lonely-national-survey-finds/story?id=58022317.

26 Hagerty, Barbara Bradley. *Life Reimagined: The Science, Art, and Opportunity of Midlife*. Riverhead Books, 2016.

CHAPTER 16

27 Burry, Madeleine. "How Your Sex Drive Changes in Your 20s, 30s, and 40s." *Health.com*. July 26, 2018. Accessed February 5, 2019. https://www.health.com/sexual-health/female-sex-drive-changes-20s-30s-40s.

28 Barish-Wreden, Maxine. "Great Sex in Midlife." *Sutter Health*. Accessed February 5, 2019. https://www.sutterhealth.org/health/sexual-health-relationships/great-sex-in-midlife.

29 Levine, Suzanne Braun. "8 Reasons Why Sex Is Better After 50." *HuffPost*. December 6, 2017. Accessed February 5, 2019. https://www.huffpost.com/entry/have-better-sex-after-50_n_1864179.

30 Dotinga, Randy. "For Many Women, Sex Gets Better at Midlife." *WebMD*. October 5, 2016. Accessed February 5, 2019. https://www.webmd.com/healthy-aging/news/20161005/for-many-women-sex-gets-better-at-midlife#1.

31 Collins, Lois M. "Older Americans Are Cheating More, While Younger Ones Cheat Less." *Deseret News*. July 15, 2017. Accessed February 5, 2019. https://www.deseretnews.com/article/865684820/Older-Americans-are-cheating-more-while-younger-ones-cheat-less.html.

32 Coy, Whitney. "The Real Reasons Why Women Cheat." *TheList.com*. November 30, 2016. Accessed February 5, 2019. https://www.thelist.com/32795/real-reasons-women-cheat/.

33 Thomas, Katherine Woodward. "Generation X Has the Key to a Happy Divorce." *Time*. October 13, 2015. Accessed February 5, 2019. http://time.com/collection-post/4069940/divorce-generation-x/.

34 Mazzo, Lauren. "6 Things Monogamous People Can Learn from Open Relationships." *Shape*. January 17, 2019. Accessed February 6, 2019. https://www.shape.com/lifestyle/sex-and-love/monogamous-open-relationship-advice.

CHAPTER 17

35 Singal, Jesse. "When Children Say They're Trans." *The Atlantic*. November 6, 2018. Accessed March 26, 2019. https://www.theatlantic.com/magazine/archive/2018/07/when-a-child-says-shes-trans/561749/.

36 Bethune, Sophie. "Gen Z More Likely to Report Mental Health Concerns." *Monitor on Psychology*. January 2019. Accessed March 26, 2019. https://www.apa.org/monitor/2019/01/gen-z.

37 Ducharme, Jamie. "Major Depression Diagnoses Have Spiked Since 2013." *Time*. May 10, 2018. Accessed March 26, 2019. http://time.com/5271244/major-depression-diagnosis-spike/.

CHAPTER 18

38 "Financial Wellness Programs Bridge Gender Savings Gap." *Senior Finance Advisor*. March 6, 2019. Accessed March 13, 2019. https://www.seniorfinanceadvisor.com/news/financial-wellness-programs-gender-savings-gap.

39 "Smart Money Moves for Every Age." *Ellevest*. November 6, 2018. Accessed March 13, 2019. https://www.ellevest.com/magazine/personal-finance/money-at-every-age.

40 "5 Smart Money Moves to Make in Your 50s." *Ellevest*. November 21, 2018. Accessed March 13, 2019. https://www.ellevest.com/magazine/personal-finance/money-in-50s.

APPENDIX 1

41 Angi. "When Women Support Each Other, Incredible Things Happen." *Mindful Mama*. September 12, 2017. Accessed May 5, 2019. https://www.mindfulandmama.com/blog/2017/9/12/when-women-support-each-other-incredible-things-happen.

APPENDIX 4
MY FLIGHT CREW

This book would not have been possible without the stories, ideas, suggestions, support, and inspiration from my amazing flight crew.

To all of you listed, I thank you from the bottom of my heart for all that you did to make this book a reality. Your commitment to yourselves and to other women inspires me. I'm privileged to know all of you inspiring women.

Dianne Adams

Kate Adams

Laura Ah Tye

Kate Allison

Niki Alvey

Susan Anderson

Jill Angelo

Jennifer Annas Farago

Natasha Arakawa

Kristine Ashcraft

Maria Babilon

Tina Baggett

Jessica Barnes

Joelle Benvenuto

Priscilla Bereza Kunz

Karen Berg

Nandita Bhatnagar

Susanne Biro

Katie Braco Comfort

Amy Buckalter

Tawana Burnett

Lori Burrows Warren

Jessica Campbell

Pam Carpenter

Alicia Castillo

Amy Cavanaugh

Beth Chagonjian

Dedra Chamberlin

Amy Chang

Ellen Chiantelli

Jeanne Chung

Allison Conti

Beth Conti

Jean Cooney

Kathy Cordero

Katie Cross

Shannon Daly

Monica Dear

Pam Delucchi

Amanda DePalma

Pam Dewar

Holly Dungan

Jennifer Eaton

Dorothy Faison

Cheri Farina Brown

Laurie Felker Jones

Debbie Ferguson

Vanessa Fiske

Eileen Flynn

Denise Gage

Azita Gandjei

Ann Garnier

Carrie Gazda

Rachel Genus

Julie Gordon White

Tina Gregory

Amy Gross

Connie Habash

Kristy Hanson

Lisa Harper

Stephanie Hart

Liza Hausman

Amy Henley

Lindsay Holland

Kathy Hovsmith

Kathy Janeiro

Michelle Johnson Cobb

Beverly Joyce Fielder

Jean Katz

Lele Keeton

Gina Kelly

Julie Keshmiry

Amy King

Liz Klinger

Jodi Lasky

Xandra Laskowski

Amy Law

Jennifer LeBlanc

Amy Lindahl

Rachel Love

Shannon Lund Baptista

Michele Lyons

Imène Maharzi

Maria Malavenda

Carliza Marcos

Amber Mathrole

Gertrude Matshe

Christine Mattson

Katie McMillan

Kris Moriarty

Taira Mulliken

Anne Murphy

Eva Nahari

Afton Nelson

Patty Nykodym

Katie O'Hara

Lucila Oliveira

Kathleen Palmer

Laura Parmer-Lohan

Anne Parris

Sara Pearson

Hilary Petit Donahue

Lesly Phillips

Jennifer Piro

Monica Rasey

Lea Redmond

Laurie Reynolds

Diane Rogers

Cynthia Rogan

Andrea Romano

Beverly Ryle

Andrea Saint-Prix

Karen Salay

Lisa Scotch

Lesley Jane Seymour

Rachel Shewmaker

Susan Sierota

Kamal Sigel

Kristin Smith Amaral

Judith Stark

Jacqueline Steenhuis

Ingrid Sperow

Ellen Springer

Elaine Stephens Pandolfo

Indu Subiya

Lisa Talamantez

Katie Templin

Casey Teske

Sidne Teske

Julie Thall

Barbara Tien

June Tong

Vera Trifonova

Fleur Uptegraft

Nicole Venturelli

Debra Vernon

Donna Williams

Janice Williams

Jessa Zimmerman

MY SPECIAL FLIGHT CREW

I could not have done this without the support and encouragement (and ridicule) from my family. Thank you. Be safe. Have fun. I love you.

Adam Mead

Rei Mead

Zeke Mead

Be the pilot in your own life.